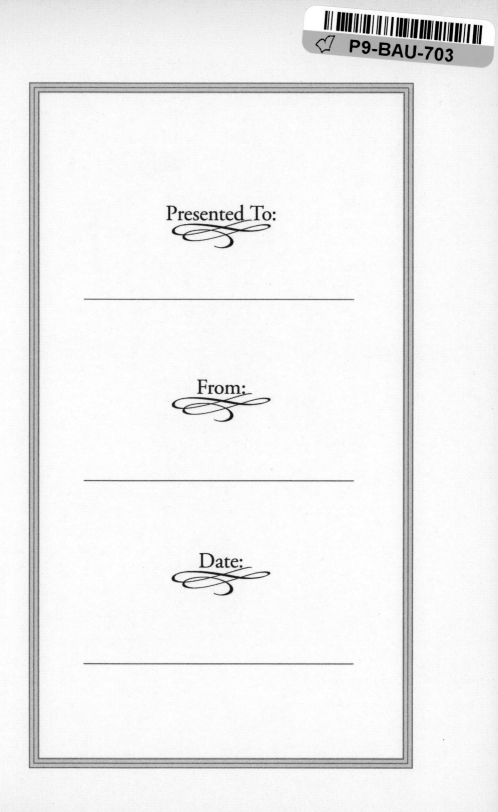

Presented To:

_____

From:

_____

Date:

_____

THE NEW
COVENANT
PROPHECY

THE NEW COVENANT PROPHECY

A Supernatural Jewish Journey of Faith
from the Old to New Covenant

GRANT BERRY

DESTINY IMAGE® PUBLISHERS, INC.
P.O. Box 310, Shippensburg, PA 17257-0310
"Promoting Inspired Lives."

This book and all other Destiny Image, Revival Press, MercyPlace, Fresh Bread, Destiny Image Fiction, and Treasure House books are available at Christian bookstores and distributors worldwide.

For a U.S. bookstore nearest you, call 1-800-722-6774.
For more information on foreign distributors, call 717-532-3040.
Reach us on the Internet: www.destinyimage.com.

ISBN 13 TP: 978-0-7684-0294-0
ISBN 13 Ebook: 978-0-7684-8795-4

For Worldwide Distribution, Printed in the U.S.A.
1 2 3 4 5 6 7 8 / 16 15 14 13 12

DEDICATION

This book is dedicated to the G-d of Abraham, Isaac, and Israel. Whose love has touched my life in such a unique and personal way that it has compelled me to want to write about the incredible intimacy that we can have with Him when we truly get to know G-d for ourselves.

This book is also dedicated to the Jewish people who have not yet had the opportunity to properly hear about this personal relationship in *"The New Covenant with Yeshua that was prophesied through Jeremiah,"* not just in a way that introduces it to them, but in a manner that fully exposes the new life, the relationship, and intimacy with G-d that He always wanted and wants to have with Israel and the Jewish people.

ACKNOWLEDGMENTS

Special thanks to my beautiful wife, Donna, who I love with all of my heart. Whose loving patience and trust in me has enabled me to write this book. To my three children, Joshua, Jonathan, and Madison, whom I also love and am honored to parent. To my father who has always loved me unconditionally, and to my mother who opened the door to my career.

To the Messiah's House Intercessory team who have helped to forge much of this new ministry direction with me in the Spirit of G-d. To Don Finto for all of his personal support and belief in me. To Dan Juster for his guidance, theological support, and endorsement; to Richard Davis, Al Sanchirico, Adam Abramowitz, and Barry and Toni Feinman for their friendship and constant prayer support. To Don Wilkerson, Dr. Michael Brown, Arni Klein, and Brian Simmons for their support and book endorsements. To Ronda Ranalli and the Destiny Image team for publishing the book, and to Josephine Johnson for help with editing this book.

ENDORSEMENTS

The New Covenant Prophecy opens a window giving the reader an intimate glimpse of one son of Abraham's journey into the culturally "forbidden" realm of belief in Yeshua (Jesus) as the promised Messiah of the Jews. Using his own personal experience along with the Scriptures, Grant Berry deals with the struggle between the kingdom of this world and the kingdom of God, as well as the more subtle conflict between man's religion and true spirituality. Whether you are a casual inquirer, a serious seeker, a Jew or a Gentile, *The New Covenant Prophecy* has something for everybody.

Arni Klein
Emmaus Way
Israel

Grant Berry has given us a wonderful read. There are several features of this story that are special. For one it is the story of God's workings with a Messianic Jew, his family, and his business. The mark of the supernatural Spirit in the account is a window into the ways of God. It is an encouragement to faith. It is also a testimony of God's continued election of the Jewish people and His purpose for Israel and Jewish believers. The story shows us that God is both interested and involved with individuals and peoples!

DAN JUSTER
Director, Tikkun International
Founding President, Union of Messianic Jewish Congregations
Author, *Jewish Roots, Growing to Maturity*
and *Passover, the Key to the Book of Revelation*

Grant Berry's new book is the story of a modern-day Jewish odyssey from England to America to Russia, and from a successful business partnership with the Lord (literally called Lord & Berry) to full-time Jewish ministry. You will gain insight into Jewish attitudes toward Yeshua and will see the faithful hand of the God of Israel in reaching out to His lost sheep.

DR. MICHAEL L. BROWN
Author, *Answering Jewish Objections to Jesus*
and *Our Hands are Stained with Blood*

Grant Berry's life story is a powerful story. I know stories. I know the power of grace to lift someone from the depths of sin to heavenly places in Messiah Yeshua. Grant's story is the same—yet different. His life journey is remarkable in that once he was blind but now he sees. What amazing sovereignty of God to take someone in spiritual darkness and shine the light of Messiah to him through ordinary Christians he met in everyday life situations. Grant was successful as far as the world was concerned. He had and has godly Jewish heritage but knew little of his biblical roots. From there, the Lord has taken him from spiritual poverty to riches in Messiah. I am personally blessed by seeing his love for his people and how he stirs the church to bless and pray for Israel. This is an important and timely book—an encouragement to all who want to know the Father's heart for Israel.

PASTOR DON WILKERSON
Co-Founder and President of Brooklyn Teen Challenge
Author, *First Step* and *Notes from the Flagship*

Grant Berry has the wisdom of God to explain the New Covenant, the good news that can transform hearts! Many seekers will find life. Believers will find wisdom. Followers of Yeshua will find peace. Anyone who reads this book will find more about the glory of God that is available for this day! It is a rare and costly revelation of grace that is so needed in the Body of Yeshua today. I can't imagine anyone not being blessed by reading what Grant Berry is presenting in the pages of *The New Covenant Prophecy!* Read and grow in insight! A jewel of understanding for all!

DR. BRIAN SIMMONS
Apostolic Resource Center
Author, *Song of Songs, The Dreamer, The Stairway, Moses the Deliverer, Isaiah, The Image Maker, Prayer Partners with Jesus*

As the prophet Jeremiah foretold:

"The time is coming," declares the L-rd, "when I will make a new covenant with the house of Israel and with the house of Judah. It will not be like the Covenant I made with their forefathers when I took them by the hand to lead them out of Egypt, because they broke my Covenant though I was a husband to them," declares the L-rd. "This is the Covenant I will make with the house of Israel after that time declares the L-rd. I will put my law in their minds and write it on their hearts. I will be their G-d and they will be my people. No longer will a man teach his neighbor, or a man his brother, saying 'Know the L-rd,' because they will all know me from the least of them to the greatest," declares the L-rd. "For I will forgive their wickedness and will remember their sins no more" (Jeremiah 31:31-34).

It is this very covenant that G-d established that leads us on from the law and brings us into an everlasting relationship with our G-d.

CONTENTS

FOREWORD

Ours is an astonishing time of fulfilled prophecy. The nation of Israel has been reestablished just as Ezekiel had foreseen in his vision of the valley of dry bones (see Ezekiel 37:1-11). Isaiah spoke of a nation born in a day (see Isaiah 66:8)—a perfect description of what happened when the United Nations voted for the reestablishment of the State of Israel in 1948. Jeremiah told of a time when Israel's return to their land would be greater than her return from Egypt during the time of Moses. The return of six million Jewish people from over one hundred nations in the past century has seen the fulfillment of Jeremiah's prophecy.

Yeshua predicted the destruction of Jerusalem and the Temple and said that the Jewish people would be scattered to all the nations, and that Jerusalem would be under Gentile control *"until,"* indicating that a time would come when the Jews would be back in Jerusalem. That return happened in June 1967 when Israel defended itself in the Six Day War and brought Jerusalem back under the sovereign control of a Jewish nation.

Another biblical prophecy from the lips of Isaiah is less known, but makes Grant Berry's story all the more interesting, and explains why he and so many other Jewish people in our day have had, and are having, supernatural encounters with their God and their Messiah Yeshua, known in the Gentile world as Jesus. God told Isaiah to tell the nation of Israel that her eyes and ears would be closed, like a veil over their hearts. The prophet was so undone by his assignment that he cried out to know how long this would last. God's answer to Isaiah, though a bit enigmatic, points to Grant's life-changing experiences. The veil would lift when the land was no longer devastated, the fields no longer in ruin, and the houses no longer desolate. Those conditions have been fulfilled in our day so that the hearts of Grant and hundreds of thousands of his Jewish relatives are now having visions, dreams, and open encounters with their God and with the promised Messiah, Son of David—Yeshua.

Like Rabbi Shaul (the apostle Paul) of the first century, Grant had no intention of accepting Yeshua as Messiah. Rabbi Shaul had his own dramatic encounter with Yeshua on his way from Jerusalem to Damascus with the express purpose of persecuting, imprisoning and even killing his fellow Jewish family who had accepted Yeshua. However, the encounter changed everything, and Shaul became the famous Jewish apostle to the Gentile world and author of many of the apostolic writings known as the New Testament. In one of Paul's letters, he remarked that *Greeks seek wisdom, but "Jews demand miraculous signs"* (1 Corinthians 1:22).

That's where Grant comes in. Grant needed a sign, and God gave him many of them, as you will read in his story. Grant was not persecuting anyone, he was just not interested in making Yeshua part of his life; as with so many other Jewish people, this is simply not an option, in light of the huge divide that now exists. Not until the signs began to happen. But let Grant tell his own story, as he began to think for himself. I've known him since shortly after some of his Holy Spirit encounters called for a radical decision. For over two decades, Grant has walked with his newfound Friend and Redeemer. His life evidences the transformation that Yeshua brings to a person's life. Reading his story is like reading a continuation of the book of Acts in the apostolic writings of the first century. The story will not only inspire you, but will challenge you to live a continual lifestyle of encountering the King.

PASTOR DON FINTO
Founder and President of Caleb Company
Author, *Your People Shall Be My People* and *God's Promise and the
Future of Israel*

Note: Don Finto has an incredible love for the Jewish people and has dedicated his life to serving Messianic leadership in the body of Yeshua. He has written two books on improving the Church's relationship with Israel and the Jewish people.

PREFACE AND INTRODUCTION

The New Covenant Prophecy has been written with two specific focuses in mind. The first is to bring the fullness of the New Covenant to the Jewish people. The second is to give believers a deeper understanding of the New Covenant from a Jewish perspective, including some of the challenges we may face, which is greatly significant in these days.

What's unique and different about this book, is that the introduction to the good news from a Messianic perspective is just the beginning. The book anchors on the prophecy given by Jeremiah to my people about the New Covenant (see Jeremiah 31:31) and thoroughly explains the depths and uniqueness of the walk with G-d in the New Covenant in a way that truly personalizes it through my own experiences as a Jewish believer in Yeshua, as the Messiah of Israel.

The New Covenant Prophecy tells much of my own life story and when something new happens, I stop and explain it, as if I was talking to one of my Jewish friends over dinner who had never heard it before. This is the story of accepting the New Covenant—not only did it change my life for the better, but it brought me into an intimate and personal relationship with the G-d of Israel and reestablished my faith in G-d.

Since our religious leaders did not accept Yeshua, and considering the Church's past history toward the Jewish people that greatly increased many of the barriers that exist today, nearly all of the Jewish people currently living have not really had a proper opportunity to examine the facts about Yeshua, or have experienced the New Covenant that G-d has promised us.

The New Covenant Prophecy really opens this door and truly gives people the opportunity to seek out and explore the G-d of Abraham for themselves, to learn more about the depths and the intimacy of the faith in walking with Yeshua in the New Covenant that was promised by G-d.

I have not left much out of my story; from my own people's rejection of Yeshua, to the Church's behavior toward the Jewish people, and even trying to fathom the Holocaust. The book is written from my own perspective and opinion, except I hope that I have been able to write it in a spirit of love where it would truly be received by both Jews and Gentiles alike. My sincere hope is that, as you are reading this book, you will ask G-d to help you to keep an open mind and that you will enjoy its content as much as I enjoyed writing it—that you may come to know the G-d of Abraham in a way that He has always planned for us, that we would know Him for ourselves. Please enjoy my story.

NOTE: As in traditional Judaism, I never write out the full name of G-d or the name of the L-rd, always eliminating the middle vowel. I believe that this is not only respectful, but it always serves to quickly remind us of the holiness of G-d. In addition for the same reason, I always capitalize any reference to G-d. Since I am Jewish, when I refer to Jewish issues, I have written this book in the first person, often taking my people's position, as my own.

Chapter 1

THE EARLY YEARS

I was four years old at the time, and I will never forget this experience as long as I live. I was in my bathroom of all places, sitting on the toilet, and suddenly a very strong presence entered the room. I could not see or feel anything, except the sunlight was quite brilliant, and I was seriously captivated by this extremely peaceful experience. Then I heard a voice telling me that He loved me, and that He was calling me to my people and would use my life to minister to them. He did not use these exact words, and He spoke this message silently to me; however, this was my complete understanding of this experience.

I just naturally accepted this experience and did not think anymore of it. Honestly, I did not really understand what had transpired, and it was not until later on in my early adult life that G-d brought this back to my remembrance and understanding. Children tend to be much more open to the spiritual than grown-ups.

I was born on October 6, 1959, to Joseph and Madeleine Berry—a prosperous Jewish family in London, England. I was the youngest of four children: two girls, Gail and Louise, and two boys, Craig and me. My childhood was quite affluent, as my father was the third generation of a successful family furniture business; and, my brother and I, who were only sixteen months apart, were very close throughout our childhood years.

The 1960s were successful and prosperous years for many in England and the modern era had come upon us. The Beatles, the moon landing, hippies and flower power, baby boomers, and the like were just a few of the names or symbols that would affect this generation and seriously change the world.

It was during this time that modern Jews became increasingly more secular; and as English Jews seeking acceptance within a very traditional English class structure, we prided ourselves in our English nationality, while never forgetting our heritage as Jews. Most people are unaware of the size of the English Jewish population, which today stands at about three hundred thousand,[1] yet as in other countries we were truly a minority and as a result worked hard to assimilate into British society.

While we were often aware of anti-Semitism, especially at school, we truly looked to evolve from the ghetto experiences of Eastern Europe, which had become entrenched in our natures and characters, so far as to even look down on the Yiddish language that had become such a strong part of us, which was now beginning to fade. Except perhaps for the prettier, more expressive words, some of which have even made it into the English language and especially in the United States—words such as oy vey (woe is me), mazel tov (good luck), and shmooz (friendly talk).

My parent's generation was truly one of the first groups of Jews to experience greater prosperity, as many of the hard-working Jewish families were beginning to emerge with their successful businesses. Success was and is extremely important to Jewish people. Our struggle to survive over the centuries, during a great deal of hostility and rejection from the nations where we lived, had increased our drive to succeed and find a better way of life. My parents, as did others, truly enjoyed their newfound wealth.

My mother was a childhood actress. She was a beautiful girl and went to the same drama school as Jean Simmons, performing on public stage at the early age of twelve. She grew up and socialized with other English Jews who were also to become very successful and famous in their careers, like Vidal Sassoon and Joan Collins.

For the first five years of my parent's marriage, they kept a kosher[2] home. My paternal grandfather was very religious and quite strict with the Jewish dietary laws; my mother's immediate side was less religious. However, it was not long after, as with other modern Jews of their day, that they became increasingly more secular in their lifestyles and beliefs—especially with the emergence of humanism in the world, which caused people to become more liberal in their views. However, we did not have much choice when it came to synagogue as the only local place of worship was actually Orthodox.[3] This is where I was Bar Mitzvahed,[4] having to take a formal exam in Jewish studies.

Being English speaking, everything in the synagogue was conducted in Hebrew, which I could not understand. And while I always wanted to know G-d personally, I truly did not find Him in this synagogue experience. It was truly a religious experience, the men who were into it, prayed and dovened[5] prayers they did not really fully understand, while the others sat in boredom. And the women who sat silently upstairs, separate from the men, very much focused on their fashions and apparel. *There has to be something more,* I thought back then, I just did not know what it was. As a result, my searching heart began its quest to know the truth and try to find intimacy with G-d.

By the early 1970s, the moral code and fiber of Western society had truly been broken down and almost anything had become acceptable. It was during this time that my parents divorced, which truly changed the direction of my life. In 1973, my mother remarried an ex-Brit named Arthur Levene, who had immigrated to the United States shortly after World War II, and I picked up two stepsisters, Ronia and Leslie Levene. Leslie and I were similar in age, and we soon became quite close and have remained so throughout our lives.

My family life had fallen apart and was now beginning to move in new directions. Shortly after the divorce, my mother moved to Long Island, New York. My father moved in with his new girlfriend, so my brother and I quickly became borders at the high school we were attending in Mill Hill, on the outskirts of London. I did not do very well on the entrance exams for my senior school (grades 7-12), which was no surprise with everything going on in my life at that time, and my mother had to work her charms to get me into the school. My teenage sisters were also affected by the divorce, and moved into their adult lives way too early for either of them to handle; life was very messy during those years.

Needless to say, my teens were difficult years—as they are for many—especially in light of all the sudden changes and instability in my family life, as well as bouncing back and forth between New York and London over the school holidays and no longer having a family home in England. On weekends off from school, I would have to stay with friends, which was also quite destabilizing, but thank G-d, my father bought a new apartment a couple of years later that I could once again call my own.

I found the stability of the four walls of my senior school really helped to develop me, and I found myself truly flourishing within my school community, playing lots of sports as well as participating in all of the school plays, which I really loved.

I always believed in G-d as a teenager; and it was really during these years that I began to try to understand the whole G-d concept and often had many differing thoughts on this subject, always trying to fit G-d into my most recent philosophy. My best friend, Andrew, was an atheist, and we would often discuss and share our most recent beliefs about things; but I would always staunchly defend the existence of G-d. It was one thing to believe in G-d, but quite another to get to know Him, which I was to find out later.

I was a Jew attending a private Christian school that had a Church of England background. It was fairly common for secular Jewish people to send their children to Christian schools by this time, as they provided the best education. So I quickly learned to juggle between my Jewish and Gentile friends. I was not the only Jewish student attending this school, about five or six percent of the total number of students were Jews. We were not required to attend daily chapel service; and we were excused from any active participation in the prayers or the service itself, as long as we were respectful and remained silent during the service. While I do remember certain Scriptures being read (especially First Corinthians 13:11, which spoke of turning from a child into a man), I honestly don't remember anything ever being spoken about Jesus. The singing of the English hymns were quite beautiful though, and the sound so often majestic—one of a number of things that the Brits do really well, especially at Christmas time.

My junior school, Belmont, had a similar mix, but there I ran into quite a bit of anti-Semitism, often getting into fights to quickly crush the anti-Jewish words spoken against me. It was in this school as a dayboy attending an English boarding school that I began to develop my business and selling skills, often cashing in on the latest craze of the day. As a young boy, I always had money in my pocket. I had a captive audience, as the borders in the school were very limited in what they were allowed, so there was always a good demand for different things. In addition, our father gave us a minimum amount of pocket money and always encouraged us to earn the rest doing various odd jobs in the neighborhood.

Senior school was different; and while there were consistent over-tones of anti-Semitism, it was always done more in jest. This was actually quite an English way to help people get through their dif-ferences. We only had one Black child in the entire school—I can't imagine how he felt. My friendships were also split between my Jewish and Gentile friends—little did I realize then how G-d was preparing me for my life, which is so often split between both groups.

I left Mill Hill after taking my O level exams and started an apprenticeship in my family's furniture business. It was common in those days when wanting to train in business to do apprenticeship rather than earning a university degree.

The industrial revolution had started in England in the seven-teenth century, where the workingman was quite definitely abused by the emerging capitalists of the era. It was truly in the 1970s that this political pendulum had swung in the complete opposite direction, where both extreme left wing politics and the unions were destroy-ing the country. The British economy was seriously weakened and the country even experienced a three-day work week. It was in this environment that my father ultimately decided to close our family business; and while I had the opportunity to train in it and really learn how business worked, it was not long after I joined that the business was closed down.

After one year of training in every department of the business, which employed over two hundred people, the purchasing manager for the business retired and I asked my father if I could step into that position—he agreed. I really enjoyed my job and quickly found a tal-ent for buying all of the furniture components, including securing the wood contracts. I would often travel to different parts of Europe to find the best woods.

I was now seventeen years of age and looked even younger, so when sales people would visit me, I could tell that they wanted to take advantage of my age and inexperience. I quickly replaced them with sales people and companies I knew I could trust more. In addition, the buyer I replaced had been there for more than thirty years, so it was not difficult for me to bring down supply costs. I really loved the challenge and my father quickly became quite proud of my achievements, especially at such a young age. I was making a difference, and this helped him, as these were difficult years in business for my father. I really felt for him, as I knew he was carrying a difficult burden for all of my family.

During my two and a half years working within in the family business, I also had the opportunity to get to know my grandfather, Papa Berry, better before he died. He was quite ill at the time; he had diabetes and had lost most of his sight. However, he was strong physically and had been an amateur boxer in his youth. He actually taught my brother and I how to box, so we knew how to defend ourselves. We never spoke about G-d; however, he was quite religious and always kept kosher wherever he went, even to the point of eating food wrapped in newspaper when in the office because he considered everything *traif,* which is Yiddish for unclean.

Every Wednesday we would go out for lunch to a kosher deli in Stamford Hill, which was a Jewish neighborhood in East London, quite near the factory on Lea Bridge Road. After lunch, we would visit the old markets looking for wooden bargains, and I had a particular interest in boxes at that time, which I began to collect. When we would find something worth fixing, we would buy it and take it back to the factory and give it to one of our French polishers, who could convert almost anything and make it like new, truly an old art that has since vanished.

Even with my grandfather's sight almost totally gone, he would get up close to the wood and feel its grain and smell it, too. And with all of his experience in the furniture business, he could tell exactly what it was and if it was worth touching. If he liked it, he would give me a sign and then I would start negotiating to buy it. We would never ever overpay for anything and if we couldn't buy it at a bargain, it wasn't worth it to him. I was constantly amazed by his abilities and thoroughly enjoyed our times together. He was an old school type and did not really believe in banks, so he would stash his money in different hiding places in his home, and would challenge my brother and I to try and find it. When we did, he would give us a reward. While he didn't believe in giving his money to banks, he did store it in lock boxes and would regularly have me check on it and recount it; and he always gave me a nice little bonus for my duties.

In the spring of 1978, my grandfather passed away, and I rushed to the hospital to visit him; however, by the time I arrived, he had already died. There he was lying dead on a metal bed in the hospital room. Papa Berry was the first dead person I had ever seen; and as I looked at his body, I noticed something very strange. All I could see was a dead body; my grandfather's soul was no longer there and his body seemed empty and void. I could not stop thinking about this, as it seemed as if the body was a vehicle for us spiritually.

That night I had a very specific dream about my grandfather's passing; and in the dream I saw how he had died. He was in his home and he loosened his tie, then he went to sit on his couch, laid back, closed his eyes and died. And as he passed, I saw a spiritual cloud come down through the ceiling and hover over his body. Then I saw his soul, now in the same form as the cloud that hovered over his body, rise out of his body until the two clouds met and became one, and then the dream was over.

The next morning, I went downstairs and into the kitchen to tell my father what I had dreamt, and he almost fell off his chair, as this was the exact way that my grandfather had actually died. My grandfather's lady friend had been with him when he died and had later told my father what had happened.

Papa Berry's passing left a clear mark in my mind, aside from obviously missing him. I now had little doubt toward the afterlife and felt very strongly that the soul moves on after death. I can honestly say that this experience with my grandfather became a foundation in my spiritual quest, as I knew deep within that there was more to this life than just the physical aspect of it.

By now my mother had been living in the United States for several years and had started a cosmetic business. As an actress she had learned many makeup tricks quite early on in her life and one of them was to line the inside of her eyes with a natural product from India called *kajal,* which she would buy in the Camden Street markets in North London. In those days, cosmetic eyeliners were almost nonexistent, and so wherever she went, women would stop her and ask how she was lining her eyes—they looked so dramatic. One day she went home to her husband to discuss this and said that she should look into importing the product from India, which he encouraged her to do.

Over the next several years, she sold millions of these special eyeliners into the U.S. market, and her cosmetic brand was successfully launched under her maiden name *Madeleine Mono.* Since I didn't know anyone in my mother's neighborhood when I visited during school holidays, there was not much for me to do. So I often got involved with her business, packing and shipping the orders from the basement of our house.

I liked the business, as it lent itself to creativity and innovation. As things were turning south, economically, in England, my mother offered me a position in her business. My brother Craig had already left classes at New York University to work in her business managing the sales. Soon after, in 1979, I immigrated to the United States, a few weeks before Margaret Thatcher was to gain political power in the United Kingdom.

I was sad to leave England and my friends—especially my father who I was particularly close to, for he had raised me in my teen years. The move was quite difficult for me; I was also leaving my favorite football team behind, The Arsenal, that I had faithfully supported since I was a young boy, when England had won the world cup in 1966 and my uncle Stephen had taken me to see a live game.

However, I was drawn forward by the great buzz of the American lifestyle, especially the one promoted on all of the American television shows that we watched regularly.

I was never afraid of hard work, which was one of the things that attracted me to the U.S., which I considered to be the last true bastion of democracy, considering what I had experienced in England in the 1970s, with some countries in Western Europe even considering Communism.

ENDNOTES

1. Jewish population – jewishvirtuallibrary.org.

2. Kosher – adherence to Mosaic and rabbinical dietary and ceremonial laws related to all food types.

3. Orthodox – conservative form of Judaism.

4. Bar Mitzvah – Literally means son of the law. A special ceremony for a 13-year-old child, which commences their adult spiritual life.

5. Doven – A form of Jewish prayer where men sway back and forth, either with their whole body or just the top half.

Chapter 2

NEW YORK, HERE I COME!

I arrived in New York on April 25, 1979, and went to work the very next day at my mother's company. By this time my mother's business was truly flourishing; and for the first two weeks, I trained at her cosmetic counter in Bloomingdales in New York City. I think I was the only straight guy in this department, and with my prep school English accent, I was never short of a date with a pretty girl.

It wasn't long before I began to put the purchasing experience I had gained in my father's business to work, and it was here that my career really started to prosper. As my mother's young company had a lot of growing pains in this area, I was able to implement my skills in order to make some necessary improvements.

At the grand old age of nineteen and with the previous experience I had, business became very natural to me, winning my first packaging award before I was twenty years of age for a new nail polish package, which I had helped to design for the company.

My mother's business was now booming, but my mother and her second husband were not very much alike, especially when it came to finances. While they loved each other very much, their outlook on life was quite different. He was a hard-working, self-made man who owned an electrical contracting business. He conserved on everything to achieve his financial success, except my mother whom he truly adored. While on the other hand, my mother had lived a much more affluent lifestyle, rarely lacking or needing anything, and spending was one of her weaknesses. Sadly, the two of them fought over money a lot, which ultimately became the downfall of their new and exciting business venture, which by now had become a major success in the cosmetic field.

My mother was both Intercos' and Schwan Stabilo's first customer in the United States in the cosmetic field, who today have both become mega giants in the industry, supplying all of the top cosmetic brands globally. To her credit, my mother introduced and pioneered many of the more staple cosmetic products found in most cosmetic brands today, body glitter and cosmetic pencils were just a couple, and her brand became famous for all the brighter and more fashionable shades that the other brands did not have, similar to the MAC of today (Make-up Art Cosmetics), which is now owned by Esteé Lauder. In my mother's heyday, her cosmetic counters were always mobbed with customers, and it was an exciting time to witness all that growth, which all happened very quickly.

While I personally loved all of the excitement of the business, my step-father and I did not get on very well, and this relationship definitely became a challenge and was one of those that G-d would begin to use to shape my character and patience. Not long after that, we had a disagreement and I left the company.

By this time I was twenty years old, and being a late bloomer, I still looked quite a bit younger than I actually was. In addition, I had no college degree, which was much more important in the U.S. than back in England, so who was going to hire me?

Along with my brother and one of my childhood friends who had also recently immigrated to the States, we decided to start our own cosmetic brand and called it Pirate Cosmetics, taking all of the new and exciting fashion concepts from the rich and making them available to everyone with more affordable pricing.

In Pirate, which was very much a brand ahead of its time, we marketed the first line of slim line cosmetic pencils in a variety of brighter shades not yet available anywhere else, which sold extremely well. With my mother's introduction and the emergence of the cosmetic pencil industry, which was still in its infancy in those days, I began to grow my expertise and further develop my career.

Within weeks of launching this new brand, we were discovered by a young news reporter, who was doing an exposé on the cosmetic business and attempting to show the public the dramatic difference between what the product cost to produce and what it is was actually sold for in the stores. Of course with our new marketing concept, we were selling for less, so we were one of the only companies that actually came out of the exposé looking good.

The phone did not stop ringing for a month; and from our combined small investment of $6,000—our childhood savings between the three of us—we realized more than $250,000 worth of business in the first year, which back then was several more times what it is today. My brother and I worked extremely hard and also learned a tremendous amount about business in that early part of our lives, soon buying out my friend who wanted to move to California.

Craig and I lived in the same apartment building on 54th Street. I was still single and Craig was married to his first wife, Jane, whom he had met on an interview in my mother's company. They had two sons, Justin and Jamie. I really enjoyed being an uncle and spoiling them, so we saw each other often.

I was now getting seriously attached to the business; and I quickly became a workaholic, working day and night building up our little venture, which by year three was producing into the millions of dollars in sales. However, it was during this time that I began to discover the great disparity in my life and my heart—almost like a Jekyll and a Hyde. I was working off my confidence and success in the day, but then going home to emptiness at night. The turmoil and the insecurity of my early family life when my parents divorced had left its mark, and the hole and aching inside was beginning to take root in my soul, even as I looked for healing and solace for my pain with a great deal of self-analysis.

In my depression, I looked to drugs, as so many people still do these days, to help ease the pain. Except today there are prescription medications for these type of disorders, which are good indicators that something is wrong that needs to be put right. And while prescription drugs may truly help some, I believe that they have become too much of a crutch in our society and often veil the main heart issues that need inner healing.

I was glad to have the business back then, as it gave me something to hold on to in my life. However, not long after we began to experience more success with the company, I began to see the emptiness of the whole success trap that the world so often promotes and dangles in front of us.

There were always lots of females around who wanted a relationship, but I usually went for the wrong ones, and then quickly shunned those who were more interested in me. Subconsciously, I think I was looking for the "perfect relationship" like so many other people are today. So as heartaches increased, so did my depression and drug use to help ease the pain. However, I was soon to find out that only G-d could make that place in my heart right, so I could even love someone the way she needed to be loved.

I would work like a dog during the week and on many weekends, but then when the sadness hit me intermittently, I would close myself off when dealing with depression and heaviness, so no one could see me like that. And I would never talk about it.

Now in my early twenties and finding little joy in my life, I started pursuing an end to my heartache and began looking away from Judaism in my quest for spirituality, as I could not find any solace in my own faith. One of the girls I was dating at the time was into EST, which was basically a hodgepodge of Eastern religions and philosophy wrapped up into a modern seminar approach. There was a three-day program with rather strict rules, with a promise of a better and more positive way of life and thinking, while attempting to free us of any guilt that we may have in our lives.

While EST was really not what it was touted to be, it definitely affected me and helped get my focus off G-d—yet it was only another link in the chain of my pursuit for truth and so my search continued. This was the only period of my life when I actually began to deny the existence of G-d; and for a two-year period, I entered most probably one of the worst periods of my life, as these struggles deepened.

As G-d's children, He always gives us free will and choice, which is sadly why the world is the way it is today. However, He will also sometimes use those choices and experiences to get our attention, and this was most certainly true in my life. However, I did discover more about my emotional chains during this period and gained a deeper understanding of how our emotions affect us. But at the same time, I became increasingly more aware that I did not have the power to break those chains and knew I was imprisoned by them, as I could feel them deep within my soul.

This spiritual seeking also opened the door for me to search out other spiritual experiences, and I began to consult with an astrologist and get involved in the New Age religious movement. My father had earlier dabbled in this area, and we had even visited some clairvoyants in London during my teen years. As I was beginning to pursue this in more depth—clairvoyance, regression, astral progression and the like, and beginning to develop some of the powers that go along with this—G-d literally brought an angel of the L-rd into my life.

Chapter 3

G-D STARTS KNOCKING AT MY DOOR

Maria was not actually an angel, but she was an on-fire Gentile believer in the G-d of Abraham and believed that Jesus was the Jewish Messiah. Maria referred to him by His Jewish name, Yeshua, and she also had a Russian grandmother who was Jewish. Maria was a makeup artist, and a very talented one at that, who got her start working for my mother's company in Bloomingdales in New York City. She was not only a very beautiful girl, but more importantly was full of G-d's presence and zeal to reach others with her newfound faith; and she loved my mother.

By this time I had become quite successful, and Maria and I started to work on photo shoots together creating ads for Pirate, my cosmetic company. During these times, we would often go out to nice restaurants for dinner where she would regularly tell me about Yeshua, but never from the New Testament, which being Jewish, I just could not have handled. Instead she would always use the Old Testament, the Hebrew Scriptures, to tell me about this wonderful relationship she had with the G-d of Israel and His Son and how Jewish her faith really was. "Yeshua was Jewish," she would tell me, "and He came first to the people of Israel." She said it wasn't yet time for Him to go out to world, which was to come later. She would also talk about all of the prophecies in the Hebrew Scriptures that, in her mind, so clearly pointed Him out; she could not understand why we Jews could not see their own Messiah in their own Scriptures.

During those weeks and months, outwardly, I responded to Maria's words with a shrug and a laugh; but inwardly, my stomach would often end up in knots as the truth of her words confronted the spiritual darkness in my soul.

As Jews, we just don't believe that way, and the indoctrination of both my family and heritage of two thousand years, as well as all the killing and persecutions of my people in Christ's name, was just a complete no-no for me, as it is for most of my people.

As a result, I could not go any further with my friend's beliefs, despite her incredible persistence, except to note that I seriously knew that she had a relationship with my G-d, which became strange to me. There was definitely a dynamic there, and I knew her relationship with Him was real and definitely not one way. This made me curious, even though she would never have known it, unless G-d showed her my heart, which He most probably did. Accompanied with her usual witness and sharing of Yeshua, she was definitely praying and fasting for my soul behind the scenes and her relationship with G-d was not religious, it was definitely very spiritual, which also caught my attention.

The year was now 1984 and our business was booming. In that same year we started two new marketing ventures in different partnerships. A funky face painting kit concept called Art Eyes, which literally mushroomed into the limelight, and a ten pack set of leopard cosmetic pencils called Cat Eyes which retailed for $5 in lower-end stores. Both of these new ventures became extremely successful.

On Art Eyes, we joined forces with Marc Bennett and Paul Ben-Victor,[1] star of *In Plain Sight*, who had created the face painting kit concept, which were popular at many night clubs, parties, and Bar Mitzvahs—everyone loved it! They had also traveled and worked their way around the world with the Art Eyes concept and were looking to commercialize it, which is where Craig and I came in. We became great friends with Marc and Paul, there was an amazing energy between all of us.

On Cat Eyes we joined forces with Bob Strom and Joanne Benjamin, who owned ACI, which managed a beauty catalog for Spencer Gifts. Bob and Joanne helped Craig and I get our business off the ground, supporting us with some great catalog orders, which we greatly needed at the time. We also partnered with Hal Markowitz, who was our sales connections into the mass chains, and at the time he was very well-connected and had a lot of pull with the larger accounts.

In my personal life, my Jekyll and Hyde personalities continued, soaking up the success on the business side, but now earnestly seeking freedom from the depression that wrapped itself so tightly around my soul. While I was growing in power with my New Age experience and beginning to have out-of-body experiences, I became increasingly aware that the powers I was engaging in were not touching the heartache I felt inside. I began to feel and experience a void deep within my heart.

It is really amazing how G-d determines to draw us unto Himself and exactly what circumstances He uses to get our attention.

I can honestly say that my friendship with Maria was a breath of fresh air. While I still carried the pain inside, it was not as gripping as it had been in the past. The pain had not gone away completely; I was just learning to deal with it better—like so many people do in the world who have not yet discovered the power of G-d in their own individual lives that can ultimately free them from their chains and weaknesses, including depression.

A number of months had gone by and Maria was definitely beginning to make a more serious impact in my life with my own G-d. For the next several months, I began to pursue my own relationship with the G-d of Abraham, as I knew she had a relationship with Him and I did not!

Every night after work I would go into my bedroom and pray. I would try to talk to G-d and not just for a few minutes, but for a decent amount of time. Weeks went by and still nothing, it was like my prayers hit the ceiling and fell right back down to the floor next to me. Not only did I become more frustrated with this experience, but it just reinforced my own feeling about Maria's beliefs not really being real; I began to pull away from her, as her persistence was beginning to bother me.

I continued to pursue my New Age experiences and one day, when in meditation, I actually encountered my spiritual guide. This was a very peaceful experience, as I could see him there in front of me in the spirit. He was wearing a monk's outfit with a chord around his waist and his face was glowing. He was beckoning me to himself, and I felt his power and his draw over me. However, there was something that stopped me from going any further, and I immediately came out of the trance, as it just didn't seem right. In my New Age pursuits, I was definitely getting in touch with the spiritual world, but at this point I did not think of it as either good or evil. This is so often the trick of the devil who can come as an angel of light, especially when we have so little background or discernment to know the difference, in a world that only wants to deal with what it can see and touch.

The devil has been able to fool most of the modern Western world into believing that he does not even actually exist so that he can have more room to roam and go about his business, which in reality is to steal souls away from G-d. However, today if you look around and think carefully on how the world actually operates with its greed and pride, it is not too difficult to see his footprint all over humanity. Today, if people have a belief in a devil or even demonic forces, people laugh at them, often thinking they are either a little nutty or quite naive. However, as one who had actually experienced some of the deception of the New Age and occult at this stage of my life, I already knew that spiritual forces were very real. I just did not know that some of them were actually evil, as they did not present themselves to me in that manner—and why would they? If their job was to try to deceive me in the first place, they would come as friends, not fiends.

Most modern Jews know very little of a devil, except only as a myth or superstition, like an old wives' tale of placing a red ribbon around our children to ward off evil spirits. However, when we read Scripture, he is a very real part of the story; and while less is said of him in the Hebrew Scriptures, he is clearly present in a number of passages such as Genesis 3, Job 1, Isaiah 14, and Ezekiel 28. And the truth of his character and his ways come into full light in the New Covenant Scriptures when Yeshua actually took him on. Yeshua also demonstrated power over the many demons that He cast out of people when He was with us on the earth.

In the New Covenant Scriptures, there is a text in Second Corinthians that actually speaks of the devil coming like the light, which was certainly true for me (see 2 Corinthians 2:14). As I was actually coming closer to the truth, the enemy threw out more bait to keep me ensnared.

In the New Age and the occult, adherents must work hard to reach the place of meeting their so-called spiritual guide; but in reality this can become much more of a snare and a possession of a person's soul. If he was able to take control of me during this time, it would have meant spiritual disaster.

ENDNOTE

1. See http://www.artistdirect.com/entertainment-news/article/
   playlist-paul-ben-victor/6062339.

Chapter 4

MEETING THE G-D OF ABRAHAM FOR THE FIRST TIME

A whole month went by without visiting with Maria, and then we got together again one night for dinner, sometime in November. This time I truly expressed my frustration. After all, here I was a Jew trying to speak to the Jewish G-d, and here Maria was a Gentile already having a relationship with Him, which I could not only see, but felt it as well. *Was there something wrong with this picture?* I asked myself. How did she know G-d and I didn't? I never had a problem being honest about myself.

I shall never forget Maria's response, "Grant, like I have been trying to tell you for the past nine months, you cannot have the Father without the Son!"

But if He is truly G-d, can He not choose His own path of salvation for us; and why would there have to be so many different ways to come to know Him, if indeed He was in fact real and alive?

"What do you have to lose? Now that you are praying, ask G-d if Yeshua is really the Messiah and G-d's Son," Maria said.

I [Yeshua] *stand at the door and knock. If anyone hears my voice and opens the door, I will come in and eat with that person, and they with me* (Revelation 3:20).

Again I laughed it off, but this time as I was walking home that night, I again recognized that void inside of me and thought to myself as I was nearing my home. *What do I have to lose? What if He really was the Jewish Messiah and my people had made a tragic mistake?* And in that split second, I made a decision that I was going to ask G-d directly about this in prayer.

I went up to my apartment, went into my bedroom, and lay out on the bed. It was not difficult for me to imagine a door and right there and then. I actually asked the G-d of Abraham if Yeshua was His Son and the Jewish Messiah. Instantly I felt a very strong wind enter into my stomach area like a swoosh of wind. I was startled and looked up to the windows and door as my mind looked to rationalize the experience, and then it passed. However, from that moment on, I began to believe. I decided that as a Jew I just was not going to tell anyone about this, as I knew if it got out that there would be trouble. I told Maria to get me a Bible, which I said I would read over the holiday period.

Business was not only booming but getting out of control with all of the growth we were experiencing from the sales of the new products. I was exhausted by this point. The Art Eyes kit was in incredible demand, and every field of distribution wanted it, from Macys to Woolworths, which was very unusual for any product to cross channels like that, especially in those days. And to be perfectly honest, we had trouble keeping up with the surging demand.

As a result, I planned a well-needed vacation, along with Marc and Paul right after the New Year at a Club Med in Guadeloupe, in the French West Indies. On the second day of my vacation, I opened the Bible, and I could not put it down. The best way for me to describe this experience—the Bible had become a magnet to my soul, and I became fascinated by it. I could still not read the New Testament, but was thick now into the Torah—the first five books of Moses—and I brought the book with me wherever I went. On the beach, at dinnertime, in my room, I could just not stop reading. I dare say that my friends were just completely bedazzled by my whole experience. However, something was happening to me that I could not describe, but was also completely drawn in to at this time in my life.

The next Sunday, as soon as I returned home to New York, Craig called me. "Where do you want me to start?" he said. Our in-house accountant, who we had hired out of the newspaper several months earlier, had embezzled money from the company by forging my signature. He owed money to loan sharks and they were after his life. In addition, all of the unsold Art Eyes kits, which we had sold everywhere earlier that fall, were starting to be returned. As a result, our bank pulled the plug on our loans overnight, and we were left holding the bag, unable to pay our suppliers. We were in a real financial mess.

The Art Eyes program had been a dramatic expansion in a very short period of time, owing to an extremely effective public relations and sales program and the excitement of this face painting kit itself, which was really the first of its kind. However in light of the demand as well as our lack of experience in the sales area, we were unaware of the potential returns of any unsold kits after the Christmas period; and on top of the embezzlement, this really killed us.

What appeared to be such a booming successful business was literally just swept out from underneath us. In addition, because of our fast growth, I never really had the opportunity to draw any decent funds from our business as the growth was always eating it up; as a result, we just looked to cover our living expenses and try to feed our business, which we thought was our future. However, with all of the success we were having in this particular year, I decided to get myself a nice sports car and leased a red Maserati. Shortly after all of this happened, our suppliers for the Art Eyes project could not understand how we were not able to pay the balance of our bills and as a result hired a private detective to investigate us. One can only imagine what he reported back to the vendors, as at this point I was driving around town in a red Maserati with what appeared to be model girlfriends and all of my friends from the beauty business. This only compounded our situation, as our vendors now thought we were living it up and spending all of their money.

In order to take off some of the pressure that I was under, I told Maria that I needed to get away for the weekend. We set out toward a French Inn in the Catskills, Shandaken Inn, where I, my brother and sister-in-law used to visit. On the journey there, Maria had brought a teaching from a well-known teacher, Pat Robertson, called "The Perfect Will of G-d for Your Life." However, mysteriously, we could not get the tape recorder to work in this brand-new sports car.

Many people who meet G-d for the first time can so often look back to a major experience they actually had with the Creator who revealed Himself to them, which changed their lives—and this was certainly true for me.

The day was February 3, 1985, and it was one of those crisp winter sunny days. The sky was intensely blue and the sunlight was beaming on the snow-covered countryside as I looked out the window of the hotel room. I had worked so hard and tried everything in my own power and my own strength to make my life work, to cause it to be successful to the point that I was truly driven by my goals. Yet on this particular morning, as I looked out of the window to gaze at the beauty around me, a new dawn was on my horizon, and I could feel it deep within me.

I don't know exactly what it was in that moment that caused me to just let go, but in that split second, I totally surrendered my will to G-d. I let go of the heavy burden that was upon my shoulders; especially as such a young man, I was carrying a lot. As I let go, I felt a peace come over me as I truly connected with the beauty of the scene, it was like I was connecting with G-d Himself.

Later that day, I was able to fix the cassette player, but don't ask me how. To be completely honest, for some reason, I was not supposed to listen to this message the previous day. It was almost like the experience at the window had to happen first, before I was ready to listen to this message, which was all about the peace of G-d and how G-d would use the peace of the Holy Spirit to be our guide to know whether or not we are in G-d's will or not. Later in the afternoon, we started our drive back to the city, which was about a two-hour journey, and Maria put the tape in the player as we were driving.

Something had happened to me—almost every word the preacher said pierced my heart. All of the times in the previous nine months that Maria had been witnessing to me and sharing her faith, there was a deep spiritual resistance within my soul, which I could so often feel when she shared the truth with me. This is why I would hardly ever eat or be able finish the meals we were eating when she would share Yeshua with me. However, this time was different—it was like someone had removed a veil from my soul, as every word the preacher was sharing was hitting home and making complete sense to me.

Why had I not seen this before? He spoke about G-d having a perfect plan for our lives, and how the peace of G-d, which the world could not experience as it only comes through faith, would be our guide from within our hearts. He also spoke about sin in a way that I had not understood it before. That we were responsible for our own actions and the sins we committed. That sin actually separated us from G-d, but that Yeshua had paid the price for those sins upon the tree of crucifixion as the Pascal Lamb, so we could be free from ourselves. It actually reminded me of the Passover story.

What I heard was exactly the opposite of what the world actually teaches us, that we need to find ourselves; whereas Yeshua actually teaches that we find ourselves when we lose ourselves and let go and give up control to live by faith. Suddenly this revelation came to me almost like a paradox, that even though my sin separated me from Him, it was in fact my own sin that was giving me all of the problems I was experiencing—yet Yeshua had come to take them away. No condemnation, no judgment, but rather freedom and release instead.

Wow! Suddenly deep within me, I had this understanding that I could be free from the chains that had been wrapped around my soul; I could not believe what I was hearing and receiving in my heart at the same time. *Could I really be free from within…could this be really happening?*

I could hardly contain my emotions, my soul was welling up on the inside, and it was difficult to stop the tears from pouring out of me. I knew I had to be alone with G-d, and I could not wait. As soon as we returned to the city, I dropped Maria off and went straight home.

It was on my bedroom floor where I truly met with the G-d of Abraham for the first time in my life, as His Spirit flooded my soul. Just as Maria had told me from the prophet Jeremiah, the New Covenant that G-d made with Israel was one of intimacy, where we can actually know G-d for ourselves (see Jeremiah 31:31-34). Right there in my bedroom, both the Father and the Son made themselves known to me by His Holy Spirit and came to live within my heart, just as the

Scripture makes it known. Suddenly within a moment, I knew G-d for myself (see John 14:23).

The heaviness and the struggle that had so often been inside of me lifted as the L-rd delivered and cleansed my soul. I also felt darkness leaving me from the occult that I had been practicing. The peace of G-d flooded my spirit like a river flowing from the mountains in springtime. Both His love and His peace filled me from top to bottom as I lay there confessing all of my sins.

What a paradox, confessing my own sins was the secret to the keys that unlocked the chains of emotional torment in my soul; as I put my trust in Yeshua, I knew in that moment that I was never to be the same and that my search for truth was over. I had found it in the Jewish Messiah, in whom most of my people did not yet believe. For indeed He had said, *"Then you will know the truth, and the truth will set you free"* (John 8:32).

No one could ever take this experience from away from me—the G-d of Abraham, Isaac, and Jacob had just made Himself known to me, and I knew that I knew that I knew, deep down inside of me. This was the only way I could explain it, it was like my spirit was rebirthed and a veil was lifted from my soul that enabled me to see, hear, and feel the truth. Suddenly I knew G-d personally for the first time in my life.

Later on, as I began to study His Word in the New Testament, this was to become very clear to me. Yeshua had actually taught one of the senior Jewish rabbis, Nicodemus, who was part of the Sanhedrin[1] and the rabbi ended up believing in Yeshua. He realized that our spirits need to be rebirthed because of the curse of sin and death that is upon us. For when we cross over from death to life, the veil of sin gets lifted from our souls as we open our hearts to Yeshua—suddenly we can both feel and hear G-d for ourselves.

ENDNOTE

1. Sanhedrin: The highest counsel of ancient Jewish religious leaders consisting of seventy-one members that controlled the people of Israel before the Diaspora and which began in the second century BC.

Chapter 5

THE NEW COVENANT
IS JEWISH

I was now thinking for myself; and as a result had crossed over into the New Covenant, which I quickly discovered was completely Jewish. Not all Jews rejected Yeshua when He came the first time; and it is actually His disciples and His followers from Israel, all of whom were from Jewish decent, who firmly established what we now call the Church.

It is estimated that more than one million Jews[1] ended up following Yeshua in the first century and firmly believed Him to be the Messiah. However, the majority did not follow Him, and were turned against Him by the religious leaders of their day, who rejected Him and did not want to give up the control they had over our people, or let go of their own interpretations of the law that they had adapted by that time.

How could we not see this? I could not believe my eyes, as I started to read the Scriptures in more depth for myself—that they belonged to me and my people. In addition, all of the New Covenant Scriptures that I began to read were written by the Jewish apostles—except Luke who was a Greek doctor and a disciple of Rabbi Paul—who were now beginning to take His message to the

Gentile world being led by the Holy Spirit of G-d, which had also been prophesied by Moses and a number of the prophets (see Deuteronomy 32:21; Isaiah 42:1-9; 11:10; 49:6).

This made complete sense to me now, as why would G-d just be for one group of people and exclude the rest of the world? While it is true to say that Israel was G-d's first-born son (see Exodus 4:22) and has a unique calling in the kingdom of G-d, who then would make up the rest of G-d's family? For if Israel was His first-born son as stated in Exodus 4:22, this would imply that there were others in the family, right?

I believe He had always planned to reveal Himself to the rest of the world, which can actually be seen through some of the covenants to Abraham (see Genesis 12:3; 13:16) and give all people every opportunity to come to know Him. This cleared up in my mind what had hindered my faith in the past, as I could not believe in my heart that G-d was just for one group of people over another, even though He made Himself known to Israel first. In fact, I knew now that the only way to intimacy with G-d was actually through His Son, just as Maria had told me, and that it was actually Yeshua who had ushered in this New Covenant promise.

I earnestly tried to seek the Father without Yeshua, but it was only when I accepted His Son that the door to intimacy, real connection, and personal relationship with G-d actually began. Not only that, but His response was also immediate; as soon as I reached out to Him, He was eagerly waiting for me, just as He is for all of our people, as well as all of His children in the world. Think about it for a moment, if G-d is real, wouldn't you want to know Him for yourself? For the New Covenant truly brings intimacy with our G-d, and this is what I was beginning to experience—and it felt incredible within my soul.

I believe there is a special place in each of our hearts that is in great need of a spiritual awakening, which is why we can so often feel a void from within, as this place is meant to be filled with G-d, and Him alone. However, many of us end up looking in the wrong direction and instead get filled with so many other things that can often be real hindrances to faith in G-d. Then these things or our habits and emotions begin to ensnare us, which is one of the ways the devil will work to keep us from G-d. However, G-d can also use them so we actually get tired of ourselves and then truly begin to look for change from within.

Inherently though, our people have suffered so much in the name of Christ that the barriers back to G-d for us as Jews, even to our own Covenant, are almost insurmountable, and it appears that they have been broken and severed forever. The pain and suffering truly runs extremely deeply into the Jewish psyche, and one cannot blame my people for feeling the way we do, especially in light of the horrific acts and persecution that has taken place over the past two thousand years, much of which was in Christ's name.

However, just as I had learned for myself in working through this resistance, which, trust me, was thick in my blood and which I had to overcome, G-d was not the one to blame for the terrible persecution that came upon our people. And while there is no excuse for the many tragedies that were cast upon us, I was not going to let man's weaknesses or his tragic mistakes keep me from finding G-d for myself. I had to make a decision. I quickly discovered that Yeshua is an integral part of G-d's plan, not just for Israel, but for all humankind.

Embracing the New Covenant actually brought me incredible freedom from within as He truly deals with the issues of our hearts—and who of us are perfect in this regard? For this reason, I now believe that the New Covenant is a superior covenant to the old one given at Sinai (see Hebrews 8:6). Because through Yeshua, His New Covenant law actually circumcises our hearts and the word of

G-d now works from the inside out to cleanse us and make us more g-dly, which I have explained in more depth in later chapters. This process is called sanctification, where He begins to transform our characters and make us more like His most wonderful Son who came to earth to be an example for us all.

In truth, we cannot have intimacy and personal relationship with the Father without the Son, as they are one and intricately connected (see John 14:6-7). When we believe in Him, the very Spirit of G-d, who represents both the Father and the Son, comes to live within in our hearts and establishes the New Covenant law within us, so that each of us actually knows G-d for ourselves (see Jeremiah 31:34; John 14:23), and this is true for both Jews and Gentiles alike.

This is exactly what happened to me—both the love and peace of G-d was now flooding my soul, an incredible witness of G-d's presence within me, so that I knew that I knew that I knew. For the first time in my life, I actually knew G-d for myself. It was wonderful!

I was also discovering for the first time that Yeshua was indeed all over the Hebrew Scriptures. My heart and mind rushed for answers as the evidence so clearly substantiated His coming through the Scriptures. *Why didn't my own people believe in Him?* I kept asking myself. Even the first chapter of Genesis spoke of Yeshua's deity, while we know from Torah that G-d is one (see Deuteronomy 6:4). In the first chapter of Genesis we can see the Echad of G-d, a composed unity or oneness within three distinct personalities of G-d. The Spirit of G-d that was hovering over the waters in verse 1 and then the Father talking to someone else in verse 26, *"Let us make mankind in our image."* Who was G-d talking to here if it wasn't His Son—Yeshua, whom I had just discovered.

I was now fully recognizing that the New Covenant makes all of this known to us, as it was actually His Son who came to the earth in human likeness and who told us that both He and His Father were one (see John 17:11). However, Yeshua was also with G-d in the beginning, as we learn from the youngest of Yeshua's disciples, the apostle John (see John 1:1). I also believed now that He showed Himself at several other times in scriptural accounts to our patriarchs, before He was to come to the earth in His human form—the high priest Melchizedek, to whom Abram gave a tenth of all he had; and as one of the angels that visited with Abraham in Genesis 19. Also, He was the one who wrestled with Jacob before he was renamed Israel. In Jacob's own words, *"It is because I saw G-d face to face, and yet my life was spared"* (Genesis 32:30).

Even Moses foretold of Yeshua's coming and that indeed we should listen to Him (see Deuteronomy 18:14-19). King David, who loved G-d with all of his heart, penned the Psalms that clearly speak of Him. Psalm 2, where He is actually spoken of as a Son. And Psalm 22, which amazingly describes His crucifixion experience. Psalm 118:22, which actually speaks of Yeshua as the cornerstone that its builders rejected—a prophecy that even foretold our own rejection of the One G-d would establish as the capstone among us. How could there be so many Scriptures that so clearly foretold of His coming, yet we could not see and understand?

The prophet Daniel also clearly predicted the time of His coming (see Daniel 9:25-26). G-d also made a covenant with King David that the Messiah would come from His bloodline and that His kingdom would be established forever (see 2 Samuel 7:12-13; 1 Chronicles 17:10-14). Both of Yeshua's parents were actually from King David's lineage (see Matthew 1 and Luke 3). There are also numerous additional Scriptures that tie into Yeshua through David's lineage.

Yeshua was born in Bethlehem as was prophesied by the prophet Micah (see Micah 5:2). His parents, Miriam and Joseph, were part of the tribe of Judah from which the Messiah was to come (see Genesis 49:10). At the time of His birth, they had to go back to Bethlehem from Galilee where they lived, to be included in a Roman census. How could there be so many Scriptures clearly prophesying His coming and His ministry, and yet my people did not believe in Him, or even recognize His coming? In fact, there were so many prophecies about Yeshua being the Messiah, it was almost overwhelming; however, when I got to the book of Isaiah, I could not believe what I was reading. Isaiah wrote his prophecies almost six hundred and fifty years before Yeshua came. He foretold that the Messiah would come from Galilee (see Isaiah 9:1). He prophesied the virgin birth (see Isaiah 7:14); He told us that G-d would give us a Son who would be called G-d among us, the Immanuel (see Isaiah 9:6-7); and in almost exact detail he describes Yeshua's mission as the suffering lamb of G-d (see Isaiah 52:13–53:1-12).

If I had any doubts before this about disconnecting from my heritage and Jewish roots because I believed in Yeshua, they were now completely gone. I knew I had come home, and I was now feeling more Jewish and more connected to the G-d of Abraham than I had ever before in my entire life. Just look at these Scripture verses:

> *For unto us a child is born, to us a son is given, and the government will be upon his shoulders. And he will be called Wonderful Counselor, Mighty G-d, Everlasting Father, Prince of Peace. Of the increase of his government and peace there will be no end. He will reign on David's throne and over his kingdom, establishing and upholding it with justice and righteousness from that time on and forever. The zeal of the L-rd Almighty will accomplish this* (Isaiah 9:6-7).

Here Isaiah was prophesying that a Son would be given and He would actually be G-d and would usher in an everlasting peace—that is exactly what Yeshua did for us. He gave up His divinity to come down to us upon the earth in human form to usher in an everlasting covenant that was prophesied by Jeremiah known as the New Covenant (see Jeremiah 31:31-34), hence the name and title of this book, *The New Covenant Prophecy—and it couldn't be more Jewish!*

In chapter 11, Isaiah foretells of Yeshua from David's lineage. In chapter 42, he foretells of Yeshua's mission to the nations and the Gentiles of the earth. And in Isaiah 52 and 53, he prophesies Yeshua's actual sacrifice and atonement in taking on the sin of the world. Reading Isaiah 53 for the first time brought tears to my eyes, as almost word for word Isaiah describes in detail the exact mission of Yeshua to both suffer and die to take on the sin of the world, not just for Israel, but for the whole world. (See Isaiah 52:13–53:1-12.) As I read this, my heart just broke as the full revelation of His mission for humankind was so clearly explained, I could hardly believe my eyes—why hadn't others seen this?

In truth, the book of Isaiah is all about suffering—the suffering of His Son, G-d's Messiah, as well as the suffering of G-d's first-born son Israel and their journey in light of this rejection as well as their ultimate reconciliation. Could there be a connection here? This is something we will discuss in future chapters. Israel did not want a suffering Messiah, they were looking for a Lion, which He will be when He returns again to the earth. The Bible actually foretells of two comings by the Messiah: one of a Lamb and one of a Lion; and when He returns the second time, He will sit upon the throne of David and rule the world in righteousness from Jerusalem, which I think will happen much sooner than we may think.

While my experience thus far was definitely extremely spiritual, it was here in the word of G-d and especially in the book of Isaiah that I started to see how much written evidence there actually was to substantiate His coming. In the truth of Scripture, I could clearly see His mission and His purpose as a suffering Messiah, while I think my people were looking for a deliverer from their oppression from the Romans. Even today when you speak to rabbinical Jews[1] concerning Messiah, they still hold on to the fact that the Messiah has to bring complete peace to the world, which is one of their main arguments against Yeshua, because thus far they have not seen the main purpose of His first coming, which was to first bring peace from within.

When He comes the second time, He will establish righteousness and peace throughout the earth, reigning from Jerusalem; and we in Israel who turn our hearts to Him will still reign with Him and fulfill our calling as a nation of priests (see Exodus 19:6; Isaiah 61:6-9). However, we will not be alone anymore as His first-born children, but will also share this role with our Gentile believing family (see Revelation 5:10) who have been brought into the New Covenant with us. This was indeed G-d's great pleasure to reveal Himself at this time to the entire world through the giving of His Son, so that all men and women who call upon the name of the L-rd will be saved.

I was now beginning to realize what a tragic mistake my people had actually made, and then the rest of the story of the Jewish people and our dispersion also began to fall into place, as well as my understanding of it, just as Moses had foretold (see Deuteronomy 28:15-68). Israel is G-d's first-born child and was given the law; and as a result was called to a higher standard and responsibility, which unfortunately we were not able to keep owing to our humanity. However, as we will discover, no man could stand up to the law in total obedience. Despite the calling upon us, we just wanted to be like the other nations around us, and still do—even though we were not, as G-d had already called us out. Our right to live in our own land that G-d covenanted to us would be based upon our obedience to that call, which is why we actually got dispersed in the first place, not just once, but three times.[2] Again, I discuss these issues in greater depth in later chapters.

Back to my story. The next day I called my parents and told them of my most wonderful experience with G-d. I told them that I had found the truth about Yeshua and that He was the Jewish Messiah and that I had surrendered my life to Him. I also told them that my search was over. They did not believe me at first, and then my mother went ballistic. My parents thought that it was just another one of my spiritual phases. Almost anything is permissible for most of us secular Jews today, who for the most part have become quite liberal in our beliefs. Jews have truly entered the modern world and wherever possible have contributed significantly to it. However, one thing that is not acceptable to most Jewish people is belief in Christ, it is as a sin! As a Jew we can believe almost anything, even Buddhist or Hindu thoughts, as well as New Age philosophies, but we cannot believe in Christ and still be Jewish, so they say, which in reality could not be further from the truth, as I was beginning to discover.

I just had to learn to think for myself and it was beginning to change my life forever, as no one could deny or take away what I was feeling inside; He was now living within me, and it felt awesome.

Like most things in the world, right had become wrong and wrong had become right, and we will discover that humanity was not the only factor at play here. So my mother's reaction, while extremely hostile, was also understandable; I would need a lot of patience and love to win her over.

When Jewish people place their trust in Yeshua, they automatically have to deal with a lot more opposition and rejection than most Gentile believers do and almost immediately have to count the cost of their newfound faith, owing to all of the anti-Semitism that has transpired for the past two thousand years. However, it was not long after my newfound belief in the Jewish Messiah, which my father tried his best to understand, that they could not begin to dispute the positive changes that G-d was bringing into my life, but they still thought it wouldn't last.

In light of the options that are now presented to Jewish people in Judaism, either as an ultra religious experience attempting to follow the Torah perfectly, which is simply not possible; or as most Jews today, just having a secular approach, through conservative or reform beliefs and holding on to more of the traditions of the faith. A number of younger Jewish people often start spiritual quests elsewhere, in an attempt to fill the spiritual void that lives within most of us.

This was certainly the case with me, so initially my family just chalked this off to another one of these experiences. However, why is it that we are supposed to be the "chosen people"[3] and yet have such little intimacy with our own G-d? The rest of us cling to our success if we have it and greatly attach ourselves to the increasingly materialistic world in which we live. As I had already discovered through my own business ventures, money, which may bring certain comforts, does not in any way address the issues of our hearts, and that's why even very successful people can be more miserable than they were before.

Four days later, I was again in my bedroom praying and suddenly G-d's power came upon me. I was just learning how to pray, so more than ten or fifteen minutes would have been a lot at this time. Except when this power fell on me and I started speaking in different kinds of tongues; I could not contain myself. It was like the Spirit of G-d had taken over and I was just going along for the ride, or at least that is how it felt.

I found myself speaking and praying in a language that made absolutely no sense to my rational mind. It was a heavenly language that was given to me through the power of the Holy Spirit. After the experience, I looked in the Bible and found numerous Scriptures that spoke of this gift and how it empowered the first Jewish and Gentile believers to move more effectively in the Spirit of G-d (see Acts 10:45; 19:1-7).

While we cannot understand its exact meanings, the Spirit of G-d definitely uses it to help us develop our prayer lives and allows the Spirit of G-d to pray through us. While I can never understand all of the words that I may speak in tongues, I often do have a sense of what is actually being prayed and it really helps empower my prayers and make them more effective. I knew about the gift of tongues, as Maria had told me about it. However at this point, I had not been near a church or even a group of other believers, yet I could not control myself—and I did not want to either, as I was really caught up in this most wonderful visitation. I cannot remember the exact time this happened, but what seemed like a few minutes in prayer ended when I looked at the clock and noticed that almost two hours had gone by while praying in my new language. And along with it, I not only felt G-d's love, but also His beautiful peace, which was again streaming through my spirit and soul.

Now I became like a sponge and was so caught up in my new-found relationship with G-d that it truly consumed everything in my life. This period is often referred to as a honeymoon in the faith, and I was not only feeling the newfound power of the freedom from my sin and chains on my soul, but His love was all-consuming, and I had never felt better in my life.

By now, any past resistance to the New Testament was gone, and I delved into Yeshua's teaching in the four Gospels. Maria had given me a Bible, and Yeshua's teachings were in red, which I began to meditate on. As each day went by, more and more of my understanding was opened, as it all began to make so much sense. The word of G-d was food for my spirit, and the more I read, the more I was strengthened. As it says in the book of Romans 12:2, that we are to be transformed by the renewing of our minds; my mind was definitely being renewed and made clean from all of my past, as well as my sins. Not only was I loving it, but I was feeling and sensing G-d's power through it.

A great deal of the New Testament was written by Rabbi Shaul (apostle Paul), who was trained under Rabbi Gamaliel, one of the more prominent Jewish leaders of the time. He was very zealous for the law and originally persecuted Yeshua's followers, but then supernaturally found the L-rd and the New Covenant on the road to Damascus (see Acts 9). After his awakening, G-d used his life mightily to help establish the New Covenant body, which was made up of both Jews and Gentiles, and over thirty percent of the New Testament was penned in his hand.

When I started to read some of Rabbi Shaul's writings in other parts of the Bible, there were many teachings I already knew from the Spirit before I actually read them. So much so that when I did, it confirmed what I was already thinking. I could not believe my eyes—it was so exciting. I was even grateful now for the loss of my business, if you can believe that, because when it was pulled from underneath my feet, it caused me to look upward and beyond myself—then I could see G-d's hand in using it to get my attention.

It's not that G-d brings bad things into our lives, but He can certainly use them to get our attention, which in the spiritual scheme of things is so much more important, as life is eternal. This life we experience here on the earth is only for a short period of time, it is a learning ground for what comes next. As Yeshua says in Matthew, *"Do not be afraid of those who kill the body but cannot kill the soul. Rather, be afraid of the One who can destroy both soul and body"* (Matthew 10:28).

We also have to be careful what we actually pray for in our lives. I was completely devoted; I actually told G-d that with my work, I did not really care if I cleaned streets or waited on tables. I was so overflowing with His peace that I didn't really care what I did.

For the next several months, I began to close up my businesses, but my heart was not really in it at all anymore. However, I was still responsible and did what I needed to do. We ended up closing two of the companies we had started, Pirate and Art Eyes, and I continued to manage our Cat Eyes partnership, which gave me some income to move ahead with at that time.

ENDNOTES

1. More than one million Jews believed in Yeshua in the first century; B'nei Ha Melech Family Bible Ministries.

2. Rabbinical Jews – Orthodox or Conservative Jews who still practice the law.

3. See Deuteronomy 7:6, 14:2; Psalm 105:43; Isaiah 65:9,22; Colossians 3:12; 1 Peter 2:9.

Chapter 6

DID I CROSS OVER, OR WAS I MEETING THE OTHER PART OF G-D'S FAMILY?

By now I was reading through the whole Bible, the Old and the New Covenants. However, I could still not go near a church. After all, from my perspective, the church was full of anti-Semitism; Christians had both hated and killed my people, how could I? Despite the fact that G-d quickly taught me that He was not the One to blame. I could now see how humanity's own weaknesses and selfishness had entered every aspect of life, including the Church as a whole, and was also to blame for much of the errors and major problems in our world. G-d has given all of us the free will to choose. Just like we need to choose Him and the spiritual life that He can give to each of us when the veil of sin is lifted from our souls, which is now the same for both Jew and Gentile alike.

Into my life comes Maria again, and she insisted that not all churches and Christians were like this. In fact, she told me of a church that actually loved the Jewish people; after a couple of weeks of debate on this issue, I agreed to at least visit this particular group. I still had my red sports car, even though I could no longer afford the monthly payments. I was going to take it back to the dealership soon, but I drove it to the church and parked close by, on one of the side streets.

I shall never forget this experience. It was an eye-opener for me as to the reality of the different spiritual forces around the kingdom of G-d. I was about to meet with my first resistance and learn how the devil works his way against believers. I had already known and experienced darkness because when the L-rd met with me on my bedroom floor and filled me with His Spirit, I felt several dark forces leave my soul before He filled me with His supernatural peace.

Up to this point, I had not thought much of the devil, as I was so consumed with G-d. However, I had no doubts in my mind that G-d used this situation on this particular day to bring me to the realization that there was actually an enemy of the kingdom of G-d and that the devil and his demonic angels, who had both fallen from heaven (see Isaiah 14:12 and Ezekiel 28), were as real as G-d.

As I walked toward the church, a physical wind began to come against me, so much so that I had to seriously push my body forward to take each step. It was an intense wind that seemed to be affecting only me. As I looked around, everywhere else was calm; it was definitely quite weird and could only be explained spiritually. I knew what I was experiencing and continued to feel the resistance physically as well as spiritually. Something definitely did not want me in that church, and now my persistent character began to fight even more so that I could enter the building.

I was to visit this church twice, and the first time I have to say I was pleasantly surprised. What Maria told me about these people was quite correct. They really loved Israel, and one of the ministers spoke to me at the end of the service and told me, after she discovered that I was Jewish, that I had a double blessing; one as a believer in Messiah and the other as one of G-d's chosen people. I have to say, though, that I felt awkward. First, everyone was over fifty years old in this church, so I thought that I was the youngest believer that ever lived; and second, I definitely thought I was the only modern Jew who believed in Yeshua.

When I left the church and returned to my car, as I closed my door, the passenger's window completely shattered inside the vehicle; and to be honest, I was quite shaken by the experience. Something was definitely trying to come at me, and I knew it. As soon as I calmed down, I drove home and immediately started to study the Word about this experience, to try and make sense of what happened.

In Judaism, there is definitely a sense and understanding of evil. However, there is also little knowledge about it, except for many of the old wives' tales and suspicions like red ribbons warding off evil spirits, or *Kinohorahs,* which are like curses and bad or jealous words spoken over other people. These understandings or habits were handed down through our families, addressing negative words or bad feelings, from one to another.

There are also a few Scriptures that actually refer to this character called satan or the devil. However, he is clearly portrayed in Old Testament Scripture; not just in the Garden, but also in the story of Job, which actually gives us a small glimpse of how he operates in the natural realm. However, the New Testament sheds quite a bit more light on the devil. In the Gospels, before Yeshua could move ahead in His ministry, He had to first overcome the evil one. My understanding now, of both good and evil began to make more sense, as I realized that there was truly an enemy of our souls.

As I was drawing closer to the light, I was also beginning to sense the opposition who was trying to keep me away from the truth. My first church experience was definitely scary, and he definitely got my attention. As I studied more, I also began to realize that the darkness that Yeshua had delivered me from was actually demons that had attached themselves to me because of the occult practices I was dabbling in.

I went to Scripture and read Matthew chapter 4 where Yeshua was taken out to the desert to be tempted by the devil. In this text Yeshua used the word of G-d as a weapon against him. Yeshua was hungry; He had been fasting for a long time, and in this moment of weakness the devil comes to Him to lure Him away. He tells Yeshua to turn the stones around Him into bread. Quite interestingly, Yeshua, uses the word of G-d to overcome and defeat the enemy's attack against His Spirit. *"It is written: 'Man shall not live on bread alone, but on every word that comes from the mouth of G-d,'"* Yeshua said (Matthew 4:4). The word was a sword in His hand, which He used to overcome the devil.

So for the next several weeks, as I was deepening my understanding of my newfound faith, when I felt a darkness or spiritual attack trying to take my peace away, I would quote and re-quote this Scripture against the darkness that was trying to come against me. Almost instantly the enemy would leave, and my peace would return to me. How was that for childlike faith!

G-d also quickly taught me not to be afraid of the devil, despite his attacks against me in the kingdom of G-d. We are now under His grace; Yeshua defeated him with His own sacrifice, death, and resurrection. As I put my trust and hope in His word, He gives me the power to overcome, and my confidence is again renewed, as I see both the power and truth in His word in action against the enemy, *"the one who is in you is greater than the one who is in the world"* (1 John 4:4).

When I looked back on this, the beginning period of my faith and the apparent victories I received in the Spirit by simply applying Yeshua's teachings and example, something became clear to me: the battleground for our souls is all about our hearts.

I had the sense that I needed to fight in order to keep the peace within me. By now, with everything I had already discovered, I was very willing to fight, as I truly wanted to obey G-d because of everything He had already done for me. I was truly so grateful for His love, which was now constantly filling my heart. Perhaps He helped me to discover things that some believers don't learn about so quickly, but the key to my newfound success was simply applying and believing it. After all, both the Father and Son now resided in my spirit—and I knew that I was never going to be the same again.

I was never a fast reader and did not realize until much later on in my life that I was slightly dyslexic, which I think caused my academics to suffer, so I was not really in the habit of reading much. However, I just could not put the Bible down—Yeshua's teachings just amazed me. The following week, as I continued to read the Word, I noticed a pattern in Scripture. It seemed that whenever someone believed in Yeshua, they were immediately baptized.

Baptism was not originally a Christian concept as most of us Jews now thought. It actually originated as a Jewish custom known as a Mikvah, which literally means a gathering of water. In Yeshua's time, there was a sect of Orthodox Jews known as the Essenes, who regularly practiced baptism and some believe that both Yeshua and John the Baptist came from this sect. Yeshua was actually baptized by John the Baptist to fulfill all righteousness. When Yeshua was immersed, immediately the Spirit of G-d descended in the form of a dove upon Yeshua, and G-d spoke these words out of heaven, *"This is My beloved Son, in whom I am well pleased"* (Matthew 3:17 NKJV).

Peter's teachings in the book of Acts is where a lot the stories of the first century Church are told. In Acts chapter 2 and all the way through the rest of this amazing Jewish book, whenever someone believed, they were immediately immersed. As I read these stories, I knew in my spirit that I had to do the same and was definitely feeling the compulsion to be immersed. That Sunday I returned again to the same church. After the service, I waited until the end so I could speak directly with the pastor and I quickly informed him that I needed to be baptized.

I did not like his response when he told me that they would be having a baptismal service sometime in the spring—at the time it was winter. He did not understand my urgency, and I informed him again that I needed to be baptized right away. However, I could see that I was not going to be able to change his mind. I respected his wishes, but nonetheless, still felt compulsion in my spirit and as I went home that night, these feelings did not leave me. So the next morning I arose early at 6 AM and ran the bathtub full of water, and then I baptized myself, fully immersing my body under the water in the name of the Father and of the Son and of the Holy Spirit in accordance with the Scripture in Matthew 28:19. I felt completely blessed for doing it, as if I was being obedient to the Spirit of G-d within me.

I was later to be formally baptized in the body that G-d was to lead me to; however, this experience was very real for me. Baptism is like a sealing to any new believer of their newfound faith. In the New Covenant, it is symbolic of the old person of sin dying (our sinful natures) and the new person of the Spirit being born. This is the reason why we are immersed—it symbolizes death and life, all in one experience. However, what counted here was my obedience to the Spirit of G-d in me, as I felt His leading in my heart and I wanted to obey.

A couple of months earlier, Maria had taken me to a party in a restaurant where we had met a rather handsome group of young Christians, who I think were celebrating someone's birthday. There I met a young pastor by the name of Richard. We did not stay long at the party, but I remember how nice, kind, and positive most of them were toward me. With everything going on in my life at that time, I didn't give it a second thought. However, when I was in the church for my second visit, in the middle of the worship time, I heard the voice of the Holy Spirit within my heart, "Go down to Richard's church." To be honest, I did not even know that this Richard had a church of his own. So later that week, I asked Maria about Richard and she thought he had a small church in the East Village and that the next Sunday we would visit.

The church was called One Accord, which meant unity, and they rented from another smaller church on 2nd Avenue and 3rd Street. The sanctuary was quite run down and very small, maybe only big enough to hold sixty to seventy people. If memory serves me correctly, I think there were only about twelve or thirteen people at the meeting, mostly actors or from the arts. However, the Spirit of G-d was not only present, but I could feel His love and His peace throughout the service and especially during the worship time.

There is something special that happens in the New Covenant when we worship G-d. His presence comes among us and everyone can feel G-d for themselves, just as Yeshua promised that when two or more of us gather in His name, there He will be among us by His Holy Spirit (see Matthew 18:20). In these moments of connection between us and a holy G-d who truly loves us that can come through worship or prayer, we can find peace, love and forgiveness, as well as intimacy and direction for our lives, which believe it or not, He longs to give to each of us. We just have to learn how to listen to Him, as well as understand His ways, for we cannot have G-d on our own terms, He must be sovereign, and thank G-d that He is.

As His child, the New Covenant was opening the door for me to know Him intimately, and I was now incredibly hungry to learn all about Him, as well as all of His ways. Then again the L-rd spoke another clear word to me: that I should make this little congregation my home.

Richard, the pastor, was half Jewish on his father's side and I guess the L-rd knew that with Richard's background as well as his love for Israel and the Jewish people, that I would be comfortable in his group. G-d bless Richard for his boldness too, as at the end of the service, he came over to me and told me that the L-rd had told him that he was to disciple me. Little did I know then what this would actually mean and how it would change my life. Richard and I quickly became very good friends, and he even stayed over in my apartment on many occasions, as his family lived upstate. He needed a place to stay after conducting services and Bible study meetings.

Richard Glickstein was a young fiery preacher who had been delivered from drug abuse and had been discipled by Don Finto, who pastored a large church in the Nashville, Tennessee, area called Belmont, and who had also given spiritual birth to a number of very famous Christian artists including Amy Grant and Michael W. Smith. Richard had been sent out by Belmont to start a spiritual work in New York City, where he had grown up.

I was truly blessed to be taught by Richard, who had a great hunger and passion for G-d and especially for the gifts of His Holy Spirit, which I was quickly learning about. I became like a sponge around him, soaking up and absorbing everything about the New Covenant that I could possibly learn. Yeshua had said that we would worship in Spirit and truth (see John 4:23-24). Not only was I feeling the freedom of this reality, but the sense of excitement I felt in light of my own intimate relationship with G-d, through the power of the Holy Spirit living within me, was completely overwhelming.

The simple faith I had opened the doors as wide as they could be so I could truly experience all the good, the love, and the peace that G-d had to offer me. I sincerely started to live my life in a new dimension, and His word and life was beginning to change and transform my soul. This was definitely not a religious experience, but rather a spiritual one, and I regularly practiced listening to His voice and His guidance within me. After all, the G-d of heaven and earth now lived within me, and I now knew Him personally—He was actually becoming my friend.

We should not be surprised that G-d speaks to us in the New Covenant, as this is all part of knowing Him personally. Yeshua says in John 10:3-4 that His sheep know His voice. One thing is for certain, though, as we get closer to Him, He will get closer to us and make His ways known to each of us in a way that is both comfortable and familiar to us. So that when He speaks, we know it is Him and not any other voice speaking to us; and much of this comes through our own experience in walking with Him, as I was beginning to learn.

It is important to note that Yeshua promised each of us a guide— the Holy Spirit (see John 14:15-21; 16:5-16). Because I had now given my life over to G-d to live it by faith, I not only needed to be dependent on Him to know His will, but I also needed to make a serious effort to learn His voice in my heart so that I could honestly discern His will for my life, which I was now learning to lift up in prayer. Almost everything that the Holy Spirit spoke to me was confirmed in His Word, and He would usually lead me to a place in Scripture that would shed both light and guidance at the same time. However, the amazing thing that I was also discovering was that the Scripture was a living word in my soul and usually always confirmed the direction I was seeking from G-d. There was an incredible balance, that I was also beginning to learn, between the guidance of the Holy Spirit, now living in me, and His holy Word, which was food for my spirit, as it always both built and strengthened my faith.

Wow! I was so blessed to know G-d like this and I really appreciated everything He had to offer me. I had been washed and cleansed and forgiven from everything in my past and I was extremely grateful for all that He was doing in my heart. So it was here in this little congregation, that G-d would begin to teach and equip me on all the basics of His word and His kingdom and here that I truly felt the fullness of my Jewishness in the New Covenant, with my newfound relationship with His Holy Spirit.

It was in the One Accord church that I not only learned all about the different aspects of G-d's Word, but also about prayer and overcoming darkness. Given our location right in the heart of the East Village, we were truly on the front lines of faith, attempting to bring light into some very dark places. The East Village was nothing like it is now, back then it was full of every type of weirdness known to man. As a result, we truly experienced the kingdom of G-d firsthand, and the enemy would usually show up in one form or another. It was difficult not to believe in demonic forces at the One Accord ministry, as we were regularly faced with them.

We had to learn how to deal with resistance—spiritually through prayer—praying against any oppression in the spiritual climate around us that we could sometimes sense and that would try to prevent the power of the Holy Spirit from being released in our meetings, as well as in the natural realm, when demons would show up in people. This was a major eye-opener for me and actually strengthened my faith as I personally experienced firsthand the power of G-d moving in the name of Yeshua and how He had authority over the dark forces. When you start to personally experience these things, you just know the kingdom of G-d is real.

It was usually quite powerful, and many were healed and delivered; but we did not win every confrontation, because not everyone was ready to give their lives over to G-d, in which case the enemy had a right to stay attached to people. This was all part of our learning experience here, as we attempted to move and follow the example that Yeshua set for us by wanting people to get free from within. Whenever we wanted to do something new for G-d in some kind of an outreach, the enemy would usually be right there opposing us in the spiritual realm. And like Rabbi Paul, we needed to learn more about spiritual warfare so as not to be ignorant in the way that the devil would move against us.

This is where G-d put me as a baby believer, to learn firsthand and be exposed to how the kingdom of G-d actually worked within this type of a spiritual climate, and for the most part it was glorious. Yet there were always battles to fight in prayer that had to be won so we could advance. It was great to be exposed to this type of ministry so early in my faith, as it helped shape the future work the L-rd had for me among my own people. However, I think the greatest lesson I learned from Richard was to wait upon the L-rd for direction in my life.

We had given our lives to G-d and we were therefore His children—it was up to Him, therefore, to show us His perfect will for our lives. Richard truly believed this and it was evident in the way in which he operated and lived his life. As a result, very early on in my walk I began to apply these principles into my own life, especially with the major decisions I needed to make. We really should not move ahead in our lives without knowing G-d's will; knowing this made a major difference in my life. Psalm 119:105 says, *"Your word is a lamp to my feet and a light to my path"* (NKJV).

With this in mind as well as Yeshua's promise that the Holy Spirit would tell us what is to come (see John 16:13), I banked these words and they truly changed the way in which I led my life, because now He was leading me by faith, just like my Father Abraham.

I would also visit other congregations with Maria, but this one was definitely special for me and I quickly made One Accord my spiritual home. We were such a small group in the beginning, and we all became committed to seeing this little congregation grow, which is exactly what happened. In that first year, we grew to about sixty members. I also became part of another group called "Models for Christ" (Messiah), which Maria was actually involved in. This fellowship group was managed by a young couple, Jeff and Laura Calenberg, both of whom were successful models. Here I also made some lasting friendships with Rex and Joy Duval, Jon Wright, Nick and Anni Demarco, and Lucia Aloi as well as many others.

We would usually meet at Laura's apartment where we would share and discuss our faith. This group also began to grow, penetrating the fashion business with faith in the Jewish Messiah—and our meetings were usually packed. I became the treasurer of the group helping Jeff organize the finances. These were exciting days when so many other young people were coming to faith in Yeshua. The fellowship was not only a lot of fun, it was also almost always full of His presence and His love. As a result, many people were drawn to both groups. It's a city traditionally dark concerning faith in Yeshua, so in New York you didn't have much choice—you were now either hot with faith, or you were not!

I was spending less time with Maria, and I am sure, at this point, that she felt more comfortable letting go, as she knew I was in good hands. I will never forget what Maria did for me and will always be eternally grateful for how she gave her all, fasting, praying, crying out for my salvation, and never letting go of me until the L-rd came into my life. Maria had been obedient to Romans 11:13 where Rabbi Paul exhorted Gentile believers in Yeshua to make us Jews jealous of the New Covenant relationship that they actually had with our G-d.

The intimacy I was now experiencing with the G-d of Abraham convinced me even further that the New Covenant was the true and proper extension of Judaism. While I may have been away from my people, because most did not believe in Yeshua yet, I had really found my spiritual home with whom I was discovering was now the other half of G-d's family. I was also not the only Jewish believer, as other

Jews were coming to faith in our group, like Richard Davis, who has become one of my closest friends.

> *For I am not ashamed of the gospel* [good news about Yeshua], *because it is the power of G-d that brings salvation to everyone who believes: first to the Jew, and then to the Gentile* (Romans 1:16).

I was now learning to fully embrace G-d's family, which also now included Gentile believers in the G-d of Israel and in the group G-d put me in, all of them loved the Jewish people and understood G-d's word concerning the re-gathering of the Jewish people back to G-d in the last days according to all of the prophecies in the Hebrew Scriptures, and this made my transition much easier.

Chapter 7

HOW COME THEY ALREADY HAVE WHAT G-D GAVE US?

When Gentiles believe in Yeshua, the New Testament actually teaches that they become part of Israel and spiritually inherit all of the covenants that G-d had given to us (see Ephesians 2:12-14). However, it is also important to point out that they do not replace us, as some teachings in the Church may lead us to believe, which I strongly refute. This may be hard for most Jewish people to believe, in light of how so-called Christians have come against our people, but when you study the New Covenant in the New Testament, the apostles, all of whom were Jewish, made it very clear to us that following Yeshua in the New Covenant, which He established through His own sacrifice, is not only the true path of Judaism, but it also opened the door for Gentiles to come into the kingdom of G-d through many of the Jewish Covenants and promises that have been given to Israel first, as His first-born children.

The G-d of Abraham was never meant to be for us Jews alone, but also for the whole world. Our own Scriptures are very clear about this. Listen to Isaiah:

I, the L-rd, have called you in righteousness; I will take hold of your hand. I will keep you and will make you to be a covenant for the people [Israel] *and a light for the Gentiles, to open eyes that are blind, to free captives from prison and to release from the dungeon those who sit in darkness. I am the L-rd; this is my name! I will not yield my glory to another or my praise to idols. See the former things have taken place* [the Mosaic law], *and new things I declare* [the New Covenant]; *before they spring into being I announce them to you* (Isaiah 42:6-9).

I ask you humbly: who else could Isaiah be talking about if it wasn't Yeshua and bringing G-d's salvation to the whole world? Did He not open the eyes of the blind? Has He not freed untold millions of people in the world from darkness and brought them into the most wonderful light of Israel? Yet at this appointed time and shortly after the New Covenant was established, the great news about Yeshua was then to be taken to the world so that the Gentiles could also find passage back to G-d and share in Israel's inheritance; and believe it or not, also become part of G-d's spiritual family.

That both Jews and Gentiles alike could become one new person in the Spirit of G-d and live in unity and love each other (see Ephesians 2:14-22) was and is the plan of G-d for His family and all those who would call upon the G-d of Israel. So how did it go so wrong?

The Gospel about Yeshua spread like wild fire, and suddenly Gentiles began to believe in the message, which was foreign to the disciples in the beginning and they needed to adjust to the new work of G-d, which was to now include the Gentile world, aside from the people of Israel (see Acts 10–15). As I stated earlier in my testimony, when I first read the New Testament, I could not believe how Jewish it was and how, in fact, when a Gentile would come to faith in Yeshua, that they were actually grafted into most of our Covenants and promises (see Romans 11:17) and spiritually they become children of Abraham, as Yeshua had said, *"Salvation is from the Jews"* (John 4:22), because He came from Israel.

Christianity is actually Jewish and Christians believe that, while they do not need to go through the law because Yeshua's final sacrifice ended the sacrificial system and introduced the New Covenant, the law of G-d is placed in a new way within us and is written upon our hearts (see Jeremiah 31:33). Christians do, in fact, inherit most of the spiritual promises given to Israel through Abraham, and as Rabbi Paul has put it, they become part of Israel, like a commonwealth (see Ephesians 2:12) with equal rights in the kingdom of G-d, as the other children in G-d's family.

At this time in history, the mystery of how the Gentiles would be brought into the kingdom of G-d was made known through Yeshua and His New Covenant. Our roles are just slightly different, which I will explain later on in the book. But the best analogy here would be the differences between a first-born child and the other siblings in the family. All are equal to the parents, or should be, yet each has a distinctive role to play. This is certainly true of G-d and His plans for all of us as we come down to the end time and help usher in His return.

However, because they now live in the New Covenant which most of us Jews have still yet to consider, even though Yeshua came to us first, they also experience the fruit and promises of this New Covenant, which is to know G-d intimately and personally through His Holy Spirit (see Jeremiah 31:31-34). And while it is also true to say that a lot of the Church and many so-called Christians still do not have that kind of intimacy with G-d because their lives may not be fully surrendered, there are many in G-d's body who have fully given their hearts to G-d and as a result really enjoy the fullness of our G-d in their lives, as well as the intimacy. This is why Rabbi Paul challenged Gentile believers in an attempt to make us Jews envious (see Romans 11:11), because if they operated in this intimacy that the

New Covenant brought, they actually had it before we did. And Paul wanted the Jews to have the same intimacy with G-d that newfound Gentile believers were experiencing, to help them step into the New Covenant—do you get what I am saying here?

In the beginning of the Church, this was the norm, as every Gentile went through a conversion process in order to accept the Jewish Messiah; they not only surrendered their hearts and their lives, but their fortunes as well, if they had one. However, today, after two thousand years, there are many who call themselves Christians just because their family comes from a Christian background, or many say they believe, yet there is no evidence of faith in their lives. In reality, a true believer in Yeshua is one who has surrendered his or her heart and given his or her life over to faith—there is obviously a huge difference here. In truth, you cannot be born a Christian (a follower of Yeshua); you must choose to yield your life in trust to Him to become a believer in G-d as religion alone cannot save you.

As a result, aside from the first group of Jewish believers in the first century who established the Church, Gentile believers are now able to experience G-d for themselves because they accepted the New Covenant and we didn't. So when I came to faith almost two thousand years later than the apostles, I was now learning the New Covenant from my Gentile brothers and was very grateful for it as well.

As we will discover, not all Christians hate the Jewish people, but instead truly desire us to come into our spiritual awakening that they know is yet to come. That indeed has been prophesied and spoken of in numerous places in G-d's Word so that ultimately G-d's family will become one, just as Yeshua cried out for it to be (see John 17). In fact, Zionism may have actually started first among certain groups of Christians, hundreds of years before the Zionist movement began to take root in the late nineteenth century, who knew from G-d's Word that Israel was going to be restored, and they cried out in prayer for this to happen. They realized that in order for Messiah

Yeshua to return to earth, Israel would have to be back in the land and then spiritually awakened to Messiah, as Moses and the prophets foretold. One of these groups was known as the Puritans from Great Britain in the 1600s, many of whom left the British shores to find religious freedom in the Americas. Many of them helped found the United States.

Two things really hit me at this time. The first: why did my own people reject Yeshua? The second: if the Church was actually an extension of Israel, as it claimed to be, why was a greater percentage of the Church anti-Semitic?

If this Gospel about Yeshua is so Jewish, how did it become so Gentile? And how did so many of our people get persecuted by those who are supposed to be part of the same spiritual family? This is all quite perplexing, and at this point I realized I had to go deeper to fully explain what I believed. A more thorough investigation was required to at least give my people an explanation to help them diffuse much of this so that the extreme barriers that had been built up could be brought down with love, forgiveness, and understanding.

As a result, I became much more curious about these subjects, as I was now beginning to share my faith wherever I went. I just could not contain myself, as I so wanted others to know and feel this incredible love and peace that I now had on the inside for both my Jewish and Gentile friends alike.

Chapter 8

THE DARKNESS OF THE CHURCH TOWARD ISRAEL

As a Jew, you may not actually be aware of this; however, the first persecution of believers actually came from the Jews toward those who followed Yeshua, who at the time were called the Sect of the Nazarenes, who were a Jewish group of believers. After the Holy Spirit was sent on Shavuot, also known as Pentecost, the work of the new Jewish Church began, and thousands upon thousands of people were coming to Yeshua from everywhere, because of all the signs and wonders that were confirming the words and teachings of Yeshua's disciples. The Jewish religious leaders of the day (the Sanhedrin who had major control over our people) started to turn against the new believers and many of them were either persecuted or killed, which actually caused the movement to spread beyond Jerusalem and Judea.

Rabbi Paul, otherwise known as Saul of Tarsus, initially headed one of theses groups against the new believers; and after his own spiritual awakening to Yeshua and the New Covenant (see Acts 9), he actually encountered major persecution himself, almost being stoned to death on more than one occasion.

In addition, when the Romans were attacking Jerusalem in its final assault (AD 132-136) that completed the full dispersion of our people into the nations (this was also initiated by the first revolt in AD 73 when the Temple was destroyed). The Orthodox Jews proclaimed Simon bar Kokhba to be Israel's messiah and savior from Rome; and of course the Messianic Jews who already knew Yeshua and who up to this point were very much part of the remaining Jewish community, could not ascribe to their beliefs, which created greater separation between the two groups as they were dispersed.[1] As a result, more of the Jewish believers in Yeshua escaped, as they may have been better prepared from the teachings of Yeshua who had told them to flee into the hills. They also knew Kokhba was a false messiah, so they fled (see Matthew 24), while most of the other Jews remained and many were killed as a result.

This of course does not in any way justify the horrific acts of persecution and anti-Semitism that has come against our people over the past two thousand years, and there is no excuse for what has transpired, especially in light of Rabbi Paul's edict to the Gentile Church in Romans 11 to love Israel, despite our current rejection of Yeshua.

However, it does show how far and wicked we can become to enforce our own beliefs over others, which is exactly what the Church started to do to our people if they would not believe. And even if they did, we were still not allowed to practice our own heritage, despite the fact that the Church was started by Jews.

I write about this past history for two reasons. The first is to give my own people a better understanding of how the Church became so separate from what was once completely Jewish in origin. Second, to raise these issues for the purpose of forgiveness, cleansing, and reconciliation between Jews and Gentiles. In these next few pages, I speak openly and honestly about them; however, please know that in my heart there is no condemnation meant in my writings, but rather they are meant to help further educate both groups to bring about greater awareness and understanding in the hope that there will be both healing and reconciliation. Now knowing how Gentile believers think, as well as many of the Church's positions toward Jewish people, I so often feel that many are ignorant to most of the reasons that keep Jewish people away from Yeshua. And the great persecution of the Jewish people through the Gentile world over the past nineteen hundred years has most probably caused the greatest barriers to that end.

Almost from the time that Rome adopted the Church in the fourth century, the Gentile Church has attempted to wipe us out. From the Romans to the Spanish Inquisition, to the Pogroms of Eastern Europe to Hitler's Nazi Germany, the very vessel that G-d had actually chosen to become lights back to our people and make us jealous, because they now had relationship with our G-d, even through our Covenants and promises—yet they were trying to destroy us.

I believe something else had to be going on that was beyond the human eye. The Jewish apostles readily included the new Gentile believers into the new Jewish Church, without enforcing any of the old covenant laws upon them (see Acts 15) because they had listened to the guidance of the Holy Spirit and heard His voice. All of the persecution is still shocking to me whenever I think of it, and indeed the Church should not only be ashamed of its past, but also how it had allowed the devil to help foster this hatred and persecution against our people, which I will explain in further depth as we develop this discussion.

In Rabbi's Paul's own words, he would have considered himself cursed and cut off so that his own people would receive the New Covenant (see Romans 9:2-4), and he faithfully endured their rejection and their scorn without losing his love and connection for his own people. What I was also discovering for myself is that G-d wanted me to do the same, despite my people's current rejection of Yeshua, which I was now learning was only temporary (see Romans 11:25).

It was not long after Israel was fully dispersed and Gentile leadership assumed control of the Church that their desire was to rid the body of any of its Jewish roots, and a great sin entered the Church by allowing this separation to take place. As a result, in my mind, this has caused blindness and numbness and a measure of judgment that has come upon most of the Church in their own position toward G-d's firstborn and their spiritual brothers. This includes much of their theology as it relates to Israel, because indeed the Church was commanded to love them (see Romans 11), and for the most part up to now, it has greatly failed G-d in this area.

Just like, as Jews, we failed the world by keeping the heart of the Torah (the Law of G-d) and constantly rebelled, the Church has failed Israel by not loving them with the Father's unconditional love. As a result, in truth, we are all in need of G-d's mercy, because in both cases, our own humanity has ruled rather than the love of G-d. In many Church circles, some believe they have actually replaced Israel. How can this be? The very foundation of everything the Church has come to believe was Jewish; even Yeshua said that salvation was from the Jews (see John 4:22).

The Church now worshiped a Jewish G-d and followed Jewish disciples and read Jewish Scriptures. *"Theirs is the adoption to sonship; theirs the divine glory, the covenants, the receiving of the law, the temple worship and the promises. Theirs are the patriarchs, and from them is traced the human ancestry of the Messiah, who is G-d over all, forever praised! Amen"* (Romans 9:4-5). Talk about blindness, if Jewish people had become blind to the truth of the Yeshua, what had the Church become blind to in its treatment of G-d's own physical family? In addition, how could they expect their understanding of G-d's Word in relation toward Israel, including end time prophecies, to actually be accurate when they had committed such sins and their hearts were in the wrong place toward the Jewish people? In fact, the Church is greatly in need of a spiritual cleansing to rid itself completely from its anti-Semitic past so that they can fully understand G-d's plan for Israel and the Church in the last days, which I fully address in my second book *The Father's Heart for Israel and the Church.*

If we truly believe G-d's Word, how many Scriptures are there that quite clearly declare Israel's promised restoration? The following are just a few; there are many more: Deuteronomy 30:1-6; Isaiah 6:9-10, 29:9-14; Ezekiel 34:11-13, 36:24-38; Isaiah 43:5-9; Jeremiah 31:31-37; Zechariah 8; and Micah 7:18-20. There has been a temporary hardening that came upon us for our unfaithfulness to G-d (see Isaiah 6:8-10), and we rejected our own Messiah (see Matthew 23:37-39), as I have explained more fully in Chapter 20. But it is only a question of G-d's plan and timing to re-awaken His people, which must take place in order for the L-rd to return, as G-d's promises and words must be fulfilled. G-d also gave a mandate to the church through the apostle Paul to properly position herself toward Israel and the Jewish people (see Romans 11). In spite of this instruction, not only were we not allowed to remain as Jews, even if we believed in Yeshua, but we were also not allowed to hold on to any of our Jewish customs and feasts from within the church. These feasts were incredibly rich portraits of Yeshua Himself, which G-d had personally designed for all of us to enjoy and experience in the liberty of the Spirit in the New Covenant, not just as Jews, but also as Gentiles. As a result, I believe the Church has been robbed of a lot of it's Jewish heritage and the wonderful feasts that G-d established for us all to focus upon Him, both in the Old Covenant as well as the new one, and there are some good books that have been written about the feasts that you may want to read.[2]

For example, what better way is there for believers to celebrate the Resurrection than through the Passover experience, which I discuss further in Chapters 17 and 18; or the giving of the Holy Spirit through Shavuot, which celebrates the law of G-d that the New Covenant brought into our hearts (see Jeremiah 31:33), which was the exact same day as Pentecost, coincidence or design? What about Rosh Hashanah, which focuses on the trumpets of G-d that are to be blown and will usher in Messiah's return; or Yom Kippur, the holiest of days, which looks to Yeshua Himself who atoned for all of humankind's sins. Even Rabbi Paul focused believers on the Passover (see 1 Corinthians 5:8). Yet, when the Church became fully Gentile and deliberately disconnected itself from its Jewish roots, it not only lost a much deeper connection that G-d wanted it to have, but I believe it also lost levels of power because of its disobedience—and as any Christian will tell you, sin brings blindness. So for the past eighteen hundred years or so, when it comes to Israel and the Jewish people, the Church's own spiritual eyes have been blinded, and look what happened as a result.

Through these acts of hatred, persecution, and separation, the true and proper extension of Judaism through Messiah Yeshua, who was at the end of the law to bring salvation for all of us and who ushered in the New Covenant, not only got disconnected from the Jewish people, but also from its Jewish roots and heritage. As a result, Gentile Christianity was born, which now seems to be a completely separate religion. This was never G-d's intention, but rather humanity's own plans, and while G-d kept His Covenant to the Church, this was never in His heart.

In light of this, the Gentile Church lost a great deal of its heritage and its roots through ancient Judaism. Even though it was never called to observe the law, there are now many Gentile believers looking earnestly to reconnect to their lost heritage, being drawn by the Holy Spirit, because now is the time of our spiritual awakening for the Church as well as for Israel in this regard.

Where should I start to address this dark age of Church history? My heart is so grieved that any human could act in this manner, let alone so-called Christians. However, the history is there and it should never be forgotten to at least remind ourselves what we humans are capable of in the treatment of our fellow human beings.

In addition, to say that not all the people who committed these acts and called themselves Christians were really Christians would not be entirely accurate either. Many in the church were deceived, especially through their leaders, who believed that G-d was now finished with the Jews after they were dispersed from the land (AD 73 and 135) and that G-d was judging them accordingly because they killed Christ.

Let me be very clear here, we did not get dispersed because G-d blamed us for taking Yeshua's life. No, He gave His life willingly as a ransom for all of us, both Jew and Gentile alike; even while upon the tree He cried out for God to forgive those who had put Him there. We were dispersed because of our own disobedience to the law; the veil of blindness and deafness was spiritually already upon us, so as a result, we could not see (see Isaiah 6:8-10). So much so that when Messiah actually came, we could not spiritually recognize Him and instead we rejected Him, which is very different from what has been told throughout the centuries.

For while it may be true that we fell under G-d's chastening and discipline, He always promised to restore us, just read the Scriptures I quoted previously. And one thing we can always count on in this world is that G-d's Word will come to pass. We need only to look at the reinstating of Israel as a nation to believe that.

Many Christians today actually love Israel and long for them to be restored spiritually and fully understand that Yeshua gave His life willingly as a sacrifice for us all. There is never even a hint of condemnation toward us from G-d, because when we are redeemed, we truly understand what it is to be saved from our own sins; and only then can we truly begin to see the real condition of our own hearts, as G-d begins to cleanse us from within, just as He promised to do through the New Covenant. This is exactly the same for Gentiles as it is for Jewish people.

It's funny, because the Church at large has great difficulty understanding how Jewish people cannot see the truth of their own Messiah in their own Scriptures. However, why can't many in the Church see the truth of G-d's Word concerning the numerous prophecies to restore the Jewish people? The truth is both groups have been blinded when it comes to Yeshua and Israel, and both are in need of changed hearts in order to know the truth about G-d's plans for us both.

Dr. Michael Brown's book, *Our Hands Are Stained With Blood*, and Don Finto's *Your People Shall be My People*[3] are both must-reads for Christians and Jews wanting to better understand the Church's past toward the Jewish people and who want to reconnect with their Jewish roots and family. Both books remind us of numerous leaders who were loved, yet viciously spoke out against the Jewish people in attempts to destroy them. This is a hard pill for us to swallow, that many of our beloved leaders were deceived when it came to the Jews and how we should position ourselves toward them. However, for the sake of healing and reconciliation from within the Church, we must be willing to face these acts, to properly put them behind us.

To name just a few, in the fourth century John Chrysostom was one of the Church fathers who was greatly respected, yet when it came to the Jews he spoke wickedly against them, which seeded much of the Church's belief that G-d was finished with the Jewish people. It is written that he was actually jealous, because a number of believers in the provinces were visiting local synagogues to gain a deeper understanding of their own faith, so he spoke out against the Jews in several sermons and teachings to stop this from happening.

Spanish Christian rulers Ferdinand and Isabella exiled, tortured, and killed thousands of our people during the Spanish Inquisition in the fifteenth century. Unfortunately, most famous of all was Martin Luther in the sixteenth century, who helped to reform the Church in Germany with the doctrine of grace. Luther sadly became blatantly anti-Semitic, which I believe spiritually seeded the foundation for Hitler himself, who later wiped out more than six million of our people through Nazi Germany.

Hitler was obviously not a Christian; however, he and many others used these spiritual ilks and added additional hatred upon them as foundations for their subsequent annihilation of the Jewish people. There is simply no excuse for this outrageous behavior and the Church should be ashamed of its treatment against the Jews—thankfully much of the Church has already come into a confession and repentance of its deep and dark past concerning treatment toward them. However, I believe that much more is still needed and the Church is in great need of a spiritual cleansing from within the heart and the Spirit. This will allow the Church to properly receive G-d's love for His first-born children, who are indeed still a most significant group in G-d's family as well as in the plan of G-d to show His power to the nations before He returns (see Ezekiel 36).

However, there is also one additional explanation that perhaps Jewish people may not have considered before, that was not the work of humankind, but rather an extremely wicked devil that has always wanted to wipe out the Jewish people from the world. While I knew humankind's own sin was to blame through the Church's history toward my people I also knew another force was at work, always looking to twist and weave his deception deep into the fabric of people's hearts, creating wounds and hurts that only G-d's ultimate love and forgiveness could actually touch and heal.

Let me do my best to try to explain this thought process from my point of view, as it is not easy to see. As I have already explained, one of the first things G-d taught me as a new believer, is that the devil and his forces are also quite real. While Yeshua defeated the devil upon the tree of crucifixion and has given us the opportunity to return to G-d spiritually with His first coming as the sacrificial Lamb, He brought the peace of the kingdom of G-d into our hearts through the New Covenant. And while the devil is ultimately condemned through Yeshua's sacrifice, it is not until Yeshua returns to the world as the Lion and its reigning King, that the devil will be fully defeated. As a result, the devil still has presence and control over much of the earth. Not only can he roam the world, but he also does a pretty good job of sowing discontent among believers and has also brought great division in the Church.

In reality, very little on earth is unaffected by his demonic kingdom. In fact, believers tend to deal with more of his opposition because we have come to learn the truth about him and he is an enemy of anything Christian and anything Jewish. Our very existence continues to testify to the power and Word of G-d in the world, and he is always looking for ways and plans to come against us, to divide us and strip us of our powers in G-d, because he hates the truth. He is the great deceiver and as already mentioned, he has conned the modern Western world into believing that he does not even exist, including us modern Jews.

However, it is easy to see how the world truly operates with negative influences of greed, pride, hatred and division—in reality, he and his principles are everywhere. Even though most of the time we cannot see him, he is constantly working behind the scenes, his influence is experienced daily by millions worldwide.

Anti-Semitism is not exclusive to Christianity; most of the Islamic world is committed to our annihilation, and even before Messiah, we see the works of the devil through characters like Haman from the Purim story who wanted to fully destroy the Jewish people (see Esther 3). When thinking of Nazi Germany, it is hard to believe how a whole nation with millions of people could be so deceived and seduced into treating the Jewish people like animals, except there be a spiritual deception behind the scenes. And why is the world so anti-Semitic today? Because the devil fuels the hatred in his attempt to destroy us.

If the devil could work his way into the Church to wipe out the Jews, what hope is there that they could actually come to faith with all of these additional barriers? And this is what has happened and what he has achieved thus far. It could not have been any better for him and his plans to keep control of the world away from G-d than managing to seduce the Church to achieve his goals of wiping the Jewish people from the face of the earth.

I have actually worked through these barriers to come to faith, and I promise you, I have not been disappointed by what I found. However, I had to make a decision and I knew G-d was not to blame for any of this, and I was not going to allow humanity's weaknesses and the tragedy of the Church's past, combined with the devil's hatred and schemes, to keep me from the truth. As a result, I thought for myself—and many other Jews need to do the same thing. However, I must admit that the devil has done his job well, because Christianity has become like a curse to the Jews and my people are truly justified in most of their feelings toward the faith because of what has transpired.

What most Jewish people do not know, though, is that the devil has been fueling it all of the way. The last thing he wants is to see Jew and Gentile believers coming together, as there is incredible power to be loosed upon both groups from the heavenlies, which will happen as we approach these last days (see Romans 11:11-15). Ultimately, it is not just about us and our own abilities, or should I say shortcomings, but rather it is about the mercy of G-d that He wants to pour out on both groups as we fully reconcile in His end time plan for us both. This is where we all so desperately need the love and forgiveness of G-d.

Despite our current spiritual condition, the G-d of Israel has covenanted with us (Jewish people), not only to restore us to the land, but also to restore us spiritually, and His Holy Word will come to pass. For when it does, the devil and his demons will be finished from the earth. My intention is not to give the devil more than his due, as G-d is ultimately in control, but rather to point out the reality of the devil's existence and how he attempts to work against us. In addition, as I have already related, we should not be afraid of the devil either, as G-d will always protect us from him. As the Scripture goes, *"He who is in you is greater than he who is in the world"* (1 John 4:4 NKJV).

Can you imagine a kingdom and a world that is free of evil? I know this is difficult to even think about, but indeed this is what Yeshua will bring to us when He returns to the earth. For surely the lion will lay down with the lamb, as it says in that favorite verse in Isaiah 11. As the Messianic kingdom comes upon the earth, G-d will once again change the rules and the system in which the total world operates—and then there will truly be peace upon the earth, because He will establish it through us, both Jew and Gentile believer alike.

The solution to this world's problems is not democracy or capitalism; the solution is a divine monarchy with a throne that is ruled by G-d Himself, which we are now in process of moving toward. Wow! However, in the blindness of the devil's pride, if he can manipulate, twist and turn among us so that we (the Jewish people) will be wiped out, he can keep his dominion over the earth, which he obviously still believes can happen, despite the truth of G-d's Word. In fact, a spiritual battle is going on even now in the heavenly realms that we know very little about. Both angelic and demonic principalities operate in these heavenly dimensions, which we cannot see, but can sometimes sense and feel in our spirits.

However in the end, G-d will be ultimately be victorious, but it will not be without a fight, and then the end will come, which is all foretold to us through the prophet Daniel in the Hebrew Scriptures and the apostle John, who wrote the book of Revelation in the New Testament, which tells us the story of the end times before Yeshua returns—what an amazing book, by the way!

More and more Jewish people are coming to faith in Yeshua than ever before. That spiritual hardening I spoke of is now beginning to be removed, just as I had personally experienced and suddenly I could see and feel G-d for myself, as the veil of sin got lifted from my soul. Despite all of the barriers from our past we face as Jews, the winds are blowing and things are beginning to change, because we are beginning to think for ourselves and search out our own Scriptures. We are also coming into the prophetic time in our world's history when G-d Himself will supernaturally lift the hardness and the veil from our eyes. Except this time, like the apostles, we will be free to express our Jewish roots and heritage. A good portion of the Church is beginning to support this awakening more fervently and get behind us, enjoying their own reconnection to their Jewish heritage, as they are waiting for Him to return as well and have their own unique role to fulfill to help foster the L-rd's coming.

As I have already stated, there are today many Gentile believers in Yeshua who not only love the Jewish people, but are also fully committed to both our physical and spiritual restoration. In fact, a great deal of money is going into the land from Gentile believers to help Israel. Perhaps the Israelis are actually more aware of this than we are in the Diaspora; many in the land are already seeing G-d's love poured out through the believing Church. Not only so, but this movement is growing and the Church is coming into an awakening concerning Israel and the Jewish people and the spiritual family of G-d, which indeed is made up of both Jews and Gentiles. This spiritual awakening is beginning to happen to both groups, as in truth we are all part of G-d's family and need to love one another.

However, a great deal of the Church is still deceived and in its arrogance believes that it has actually replaced Israel (see Romans 11:20-21). This doctrine is called "Replacement Theology" and is unfortunately fueled by the Church's disconnection and all of its anti-Semitism toward our people. I believe G-d has given them over to a deception until they repent of this evil belief that denies G-d's word to His physical first-born children who have suffered more than all the other peoples on the earth for the kingdom of G-d to be established. In Isaiah's words:

> Comfort, comfort my people, says your G-d. Speak tenderly to Jerusalem and proclaim to her that her hard service has been completed, that her sin has been paid for, that she has received from the L-rd's hand double for all her sins (Isaiah 40:1-2).

Since I was beginning to understand the whole picture better between both Jew and Gentile, it also freed me to really love all of G-d's family and to work on any issues in my own heart that may have fostered any division or judgment between the two groups. I believe that G-d truly wants to reconnect us and that His love will compel us to become one in the Spirit, as Yeshua Himself cried out for, as it is written about by the apostle John in chapter 17. However, there is much for both groups to address from our pasts for this healing to take place, as Shakespeare said, "To err is human, to forgive divine." As deep as many of these wounds go in our hearts, there is nothing that G-d cannot touch and heal, if we will are willing.

To my Gentile believing family reading this book, would you consider seeking forgiveness from your ancestral past toward the Jewish people along with the slightest hint of replacement theology, thinking that the Church has replaced Israel, so this healing and cleansing can begin to take place? And to my Jewish family, would you be willing to forgive the Church's dark past toward our people in their hope and desire to reconnect to us?

ENDNOTES

1. Simon bar Kokhba, visit http://www.newworldencyclopedia. org/entry/Simon_Bar_Kochba for more information.

2. *The Feasts of Adonai* by Valerie Moody; *Christ in the Passover* by Moishe Rosen.

3. Don Finto, *Your People Shall Be My People: How Israel, the Jews, and the Christian Church will Come Together in the Last Days* (Ventura, CA: Regal Books, 2001).

Chapter 9

ISRAEL IS YOUR HOME

Back to my story...

As I continued to read the Bible, I was drawn back to Israel in my spirit, and I longed to revisit the land as a believer in Yeshua. I had been to Israel in 1978, which was the first vacation trip I ever took on my own. I absolutely loved it and even thought of living there, but knew it would not be easy to make a living at that time.

So I decided to revisit Israel. I really wanted my trip to be as spiritual as possible, so I started to fast for it; I had learned the principles of fasting from Richard, who was also quite disciplined in this area. I started to view this journey as a spiritual adventure and earnestly looked to connect with G-d through my visit back to the land. Almost every day for three months, I prayed that I would experience a visitation of Yeshua while I was in Israel.

It was now July 1985, and I had finished closing two of the companies that I was operating. I thanked G-d that we managed to avoid bankruptcy so my brother and I would be free to move on with our lives. I still had a little money left in my savings, so I decided to take the summer off and travel, as I really needed a good break. On the way to Israel I stopped off in Italy to visit some friends and do some sightseeing in Venice and Rome, and I visited the Vatican. I was amazed at all of the incredible art that depicted the life of Christ and the apostles, but was quite surprised by how Gentile they had depicted Him. When inquiring of the Spirit about the Roman Catholic Church, which controlled much of early Christianity and also seemed very religious, He quickly reminded me how easy it was for those in power to fall into legalism, just like the Pharisees who were the religious leaders of Yeshua's time. And I prayed for the Roman Catholic Church and all of its followers that G-d would bless them with more of the intimacy with the Holy Spirit from the New Covenant, as well as a greater individual knowledge for each Catholic to know G-d's Word for themselves.

From Italy, I went straight to Israel to start my journey—and what a visit it turned out to be. I centered out of Jerusalem for the first part and went north to the Sea of Galilee to see where Yeshua had started His ministry. I found myself reading the Beatitudes on the Galilean mountainside to the group that I was traveling with. Back in Jerusalem, I visited all of the sites where Yeshua had been; on my second day there, I rose early to visit the Wailing Wall for prayer, and I had decided to fast. When I arrived at the Wall, I was immediately met by Orthodox Jews who asked me if I was Jewish or Christian, to which I answered, "I'm Jewish, and I believe Yeshua is the Messiah." They did not care for my answer. As I laid my hands on the Wall and started to pray quietly in tongues, I felt the pain of my people and began to weep in the spirit as well as pray for the Jewish men who had just approached me, that G-d would remove the religious veil from their eyes so that they could see and hear the truth about Yeshua, who is really their Messiah, too!

After the Wall, I visited the Dome of the Rock—the Muslim mosque that sits on the very place where Abraham offered up Isaac to G-d. I was not pleased with this and wanted to know why Islam had taken this place from Israel. I later found out that the Muslims are told that this is the exact same place where Abraham offered Ishmael, the son he had with Hagar, Sarah's maidservant, which is simply not true. I did not go into any of the three buildings on the Temple Mount; however, feeling led by the Spirit, I was reminded of Israel's victory over Jericho (see Joshua 6) and how G-d had led them to walk around the city walls seven times. So I started to do the same, reclaiming this land for Yeshua and for Israel.

As I started my fourth rotation, I was suddenly seized by three guards and taken to a security office where I was questioned for several minutes about my background and visit. I was not completely honest with my answers, as I did not want them to know what I was doing and tried to say as little as possible, except that I was a tourist from the United States and wanted to walk on the grounds. They eventually let me go, however they would not let me get close to the main Dome, and they kept my passport, which made me nervous.

After they let me go, I still felt determined to finish the seven rotations and now decided to broaden my walk around the entire property, as I could no longer get close to the Dome of the Rock. So I walked another three and half times around the property. I took my time now, so as not to make it obvious what I was doing. As soon as I was finished, I went back to the desk where my passport was being held; after several minutes of waiting, they returned it to me. However, I had told them the address of the hotel where I was staying and this worried me. I was now afraid that they would come after me, especially in light of not giving them truthful answers. Fear came over me, and I broke my fast, smoked a cigarette, and drank a coca cola. I returned to the hotel as quickly as I could, packed my bags, and got on a bus headed as far south as possible, which was toward Eilat.

Once on the bus and in reflection, I was quite disappointed that I broke my fast and had allowed fear to take over; how spiritual could I be? However, I have to say that I was really pleased to be out of there and did not return to Jerusalem until the end of my visit, about ten days later. I found the desert beauty and its stillness quite remarkable, not something we Westerners often experience. This was not my first visit to the desert; here I was looking to get as close to Horeb as possible. Horeb was the mountain in the Sinai where G-d had given Moses the Ten Commandments and it was in this place that I was sincerely hoping and praying to meet with G-d. We don't get if we do not ask, and my childlike faith was now truly expectant of something on this mountain.

As soon as I got to Eilat, I made inquiries about going farther south to Sinai and found a tour that advertised that the participants could actually climb Horeb and camp out overnight on the special mountaintop. No one is certain if this was the actual mountain that Moses was on or not. However, it was the best and closest that I could get, so I jumped on it and planned the journey in the next couple of days. In the meantime, I found a nice little hotel in the town of Eilat, the southern most city in Israel, right on the tip of the Red Sea. The town was very small and just beginning to develop, but I really enjoyed the area, the beaches, and the scuba diving in the Red Sea, which was truly magnificent. I have never been surrounded by so many tropical fish that were quite uninhibited by our closeness; they seemed to be aware that we were not allowed to touch them.

We began our journey early in the morning and drove several hours into the Sinai desert. There was a peace agreement in place at that time between Israel and Egypt, which was made between Prime Minister Menachem Begin of Israel and President Anwar Sadat of Egypt, who paid dearly for this with an assassination of his life in 1981. And so we were allowed to travel south, deep into the Sinai desert. We arrived around lunchtime and started our climb up the mountain toward the end of the afternoon after the heat of day had passed. The mountain range was beautiful and quite steep, it was very arid, and the sun filled a brilliant blue sky.

The hike took us a couple of hours as we meandered through the rocky, creviced path. We stopped to eat our sandwiches along the way before we began the steeper part of the trail, which took us about an hour to complete. However, we did not go to the top, but rather stopped and stationed ourselves for the night a few hundred feet below. I was quite disappointed by this, so I inquired about it with our guide who informed me that this was the planned rest area for the night. As a result, I decided to go up to the top on my own.

By now it was beginning to get dark, but there was just enough light from the twilight-lit sky for me to see where I was going, so I quickly moved ahead to make it to the top in time. It was suddenly very quiet and I, of course, was not used to the noises of the desert that I heard around me from time to time. By the time I made it to the top, it was almost completely dark. The trail seemed never-ending and I felt like I would not make it, but there was still a little light to see where I was going from the starry-filled sky. In this part of the world with no city lights, I could see thousands upon thousands of stars, and here I truly related to the conversation that G-d had with Abraham, when He said that his descendants would be more numerous than all of the stars in the sky.

I was quite thankful that the starry sky was shedding some light around my path, so I could at least see a little bit of what was around me. I also have to honest, with the occasional desert noises and the darkness around me, I was a little scared. However, I was also determined to make it to the top so I could pray. I was hungry to meet with G-d and here of all places, the very mountain where G-d had given the law to Moses, I was truly excited—the adrenalin was pumping.

I reached a plateau that seemed to be as close to the top as I was going to get, and there I rested. There were rocks all around me; however, ahead of me was a slope that declined for about one hundred feet. On the right side was the beginning of a rock wall, and farther along it, there was what appeared to be a small cave in the wall. I knew that I had gone too far to head back to camp for the night, so I sat down and started to pray in tongues, and then I fell asleep.

In my sleep I had an incredible dream, or in this case maybe it was a vision within a dream, and it was very clear. I had awakened and there was an incredibly bright light shining out of the cave on the right side of the rock wall. I got up and went toward the light; and when I got there, the light was even more intense, beaming out of the cave. Not only was I acting cautiously, but I was also somewhat fearful as I peeked my head inside the cave. Suddenly to my amazement there before me was Yeshua standing in the middle of the cave with His arms beckoning toward me. I could not see His face, but the brilliance of the light shone from every part of His being—the cave was completely filled with His presence and His glory, for He was truly awesome. However, within the vision, I was still feeling the fear from all of the desert noises and the silence of the night, and I did not go in. That is all I could remember of the dream vision when I woke up.

After I got over my disappointment for being fearful, I was incredibly blessed with what G-d had shown me. He truly answered all of my prayers, as my desire was to see Him and, of course, I have never forgotten this amazing experience. When I awoke, I started to hear other voices, and I decided to move very slowly toward them, they may have been a few hundred yards away from me. When I got there, I was pleased to discover a number of others who had made the same journey as me to the top. Here we all sat along a seat in the rock, right before a steep precipice that was completely safe, so we were ready to witness the sunrise as it came up on the mountain of Horeb, which surely did not disappoint us—the brilliance of the sunrise touched our spirits. It had truly been a wonderful experience and my spirit was filled with His presence, especially after the fear had gone.

After Israel, I completed my journey by visiting my father for a couple of weeks in Southern Spain, in Marbella where he lived after emigrating there from England when he retired in 1979. This finished off a wonderful summer vacation that I was well in need of after everything I had experienced with the loss of my business.

Chapter 10

G-D TURNED FOURTEEN INTO
FOUR HUNDRED

After returning home that summer, I again immersed myself in as many spiritual meetings as I could attend, both at One Accord and the Models ministry, and the L-rd was adding to our numbers others who were coming to Yeshua in both groups.

Richard had truly emphasized the liberty we had in the Spirit and that we must be led by the Holy Spirit in all that we do. However, I was still smoking cigarettes and had felt no leading or direction to give them up, until this point. I think in our walks with Messiah, He does not like us to have any addictions or any idols that can come before Him; just look at the first two commandments (see Exodus 20:3-6).

I was just about to encounter my first major trial, as one day Richard made a comment to me about smoking, and I knew the L-rd was using him, as I now felt G-d's conviction in my spirit and my peace had gone. I went home and prayed and asked the L-rd to forgive me for this addiction. I confessed it to Him and asked Him for the strength to overcome it and let it go! This was my first major test and indeed it became a struggle. For several days I went back and forth, throwing out many new cigarette packs, but usually always giving in to the temptation and buying another.

About ten days after I started this battle, I distinctly remember being really disappointed in myself and throwing away another pack of cigarettes into a trash bin on 2nd Avenue and yelling out, "Enough! No more in Yeshua's name." From that moment, I was clean and moved on to receive my victory from the smoking addiction that had controlled my life for some twelve years. I had started to smoke when I was thirteen years of age. Praise G-d for His strength.

There is a Scripture in the Gospels that really helped me with this trial, where Yeshua had told His disciples that if anyone would come after Him, he must deny himself, pick up the crucifixion tree, and follow Him (see Luke 9:23), and this was certainly very true for me. However, I had to surrender first, before I could find the freedom on the other side of the tree, which is so true of many of the trials we experience in both life and our walks with G-d, who in reality is using this life to prepare us for an eternity with Him.

Wow, we have so much to look forward to as believers, and there is such incredible power in both the tree of crucifixion and the resurrection in each of our lives. Often our own will to surrender different issues and trials of our hearts leads to new life and victories that only this denial and process can provide. (The world tells us that we need to find ourselves, whereas in the Kingdom, this is only possible when we lose ourselves to faith; it is actually the complete opposite.) However, this is sad for those who do not believe in G-d, as they have nothing to believe in beyond this life and the veil of sin clouds their perception from the truth, which also prevents them from seeing clearly. The good news about Yeshua in the New Covenant, is that the power of G-d is there for all those who believe: first for the Jew, then for the Gentile, but it is foolishness to those who are perishing, because without their sin being removed they are still blind to the truth (see Romans 1:16; 1 Corinthians 1:18).

However, I also knew that it was only by His grace that I could now see and that He removed the veil from my own heart, which would always give me more patience and compassion to be able to reach out to others in the world if they have not yet had this experience. Yeshua told a story, known as the parable of the workers, which tells us that believers come into the kingdom at different times, some at the beginning, some in the middle, and some at the end of their lives. We never know, only G-d knows (see Matthew 20:1-16).

I was so thrilled and overflowing with G-d's love and power in my life that I truly wanted to dedicate the rest of my life to serving Him. I continued joining Richard on his ministry trips, and over the next several months we visited a number of conferences given by a teacher named John Wimber who definitely had a gift from G-d to teach others how to move in the gifts and power of the Holy Spirit (see 1 Corinthians 12). None of this seemed a stretch for me, as I had just read the book of Acts; and indeed John Wimber would teach us how to move in the same gifts that the apostles moved in. I can honestly say that I thought this was the norm, or should be. After all, why wouldn't the body want to move in the gifts of the Holy Spirit, as it was quite clear from Scripture that they were to both advance and demonstrate the kingdom.

It was not until later that I began to understand that some people in the body were fearful of the gifts, as they were never sure whose power was behind the activity, G-d or the devil. So respectfully some in the body are much more conservative in interpreting these areas of Scripture and theology. And I was beginning to find out that G-d is very respectful to each of us in what we actually believe and that love should always help us overcome our differences. After all, as a Jew, I was now in the Church that over the past nineteen hundred years had actually persecuted my own people; and to be honest, I really needed

His love to help me overcome this, which He provided for me. The L-rd is always there for us to do His will upon the earth, which is to love one another above everything, including most of our theological differences. For the sake of unity in the family of G-d, can we not agree to disagree and still focus on the basic fundamentals of the faith as children of G-d? For ultimately, Yeshua has told us that we will be known by the love that we have for one another (see John 13:34).

We so easily blame G-d for bad things that happen in our world, when ultimately we don't really accept responsibility for our own actions; it was becoming quite obvious to me that G-d had given us the free will to chose, and that nearly all the problems in the world stem from ourselves, not from G-d.

From the beginning of my relationship with G-d, I always wanted His fullness, which in my mind included all of the gifts of the Holy Spirit, so I was hungry for them. I think the big problem we have with moving out into the spiritual realm is because we can so easily get carried away in these areas and can move us into what the New Testament calls our flesh—our own wills and nature—rather than operating fully under the Spirit, which is not easy to do.

During this time, there is no question that in my own life this is exactly what happened to me as I started to move out in the power of G-d without a more solid foundation in my life. After all, I had only just become a new believer, and what I really needed and still need every day of my life, is more of His character and His word in me, something that only time, patience, and maturity can bring to pass. However, this does not mean that we should discard the gifts of G-d, but rather yield to Him in greater trust and dependency in the hope of developing that character within us to balance it out.

Having said that, I would never want to replace this time in my life and all that I learned about the power and gifts of the Holy Spirit. I still believe that we must work with the Holy Spirit and come into more agreement with Him so that He can move more powerfully in our lives and especially in the lives of those who are around us, so that the kingdom would be demonstrated more effectively and that the harvest will truly be impacted by it.

One Accord was a great place of fellowship, as our group was full of young and vibrant Jewish and Gentile believers, most of whom were from the arts world, and we truly enjoyed each others' company and loved what G-d was doing in our lives. The love of G-d was always present, which I believe G-d used to draw others to Himself.

A number of us liked to ski and Richard would get inexpensive ski tickets from Potter Brothers in upstate New York. A few of us decided to join him. On this particular occasion as we were driving to the Mountain, Richard lost his wallet, his money, as well as our ski tickets at one of the toll booths on the journey. We discovered the loss a half hour before we got the slopes. Everyone was quite disappointed; it seemed that our only option was to turn around and go home. Then I prayed, and we asked G-d to get a hold of the wallet and somehow to return it to us. After that, we decided to finish the journey to the ski mountain, just in case, as we were not that far anyway.

When we arrived, Richard went to the ticket office to see if he could work something out. As G-d would have it, a person came up to Richard as he was explaining the situation to the people in the office and returned his wallet to him. The person had picked it up right by the toll stop where he had dropped it and by chance was driving to the same place. Can you imagine that? The odds of this happening were incredibly slim, all those miles away. We were all overjoyed and amazed as to how G-d had answered our prayers. Ever since that experience, I have always had faith to pray for missing things around me, as G-d sees everything. Just ask my children about this; whenever we cannot find something, the first thing I always tell them is to pray and ask G-d, who sees everything.

This is faith operating into small things, but I can assure you that He can handle it and that we don't have to worry about bothering G-d. This is a great misconception of us putting our own limitations on an all-powerful and consuming G-d, who has created everything we can see feel or touch within our entire universe. In fact, His being is so beyond our comprehension, yet He loves to be involved in the tiniest of details in each of our lives and takes joy in it as well, so ask away!

After attending a couple of the Wimber conferences, we brought these teachings back to One Accord, and they truly made an impact in our ministry and worship. With Richard's support, I started to reach out to homeless men. I went downtown to a small mission house called the Bowery Mission, where I began to preach one Sunday a month. Shortly after, others from the congregation joined me in this outreach, which we continued for more than five years. Earlier that year, in the spring when I started this work, I would drive in my red Maserati to the mission to pick up some of the men whom we were ministering to, and bring them back to One Accord for the evening service. You would have to see this to believe it. Homeless men driving off in a luxury Italian sports car, and what was even more remarkable was that I never even gave it a second thought or worried that something may happen. Talk about blind faith!

We did have some occasional theft problems at One Accord, as we were always trying to reach out to whomever would listen, but I can tell you, it was never from any of homeless men from the Bowery. I believe G-d's grace was upon us for reaching out to these men who we hoped could find a second chance in life, and some of them did.

We also started a street ministry and would often go out on the streets on Sundays before service. This is where G-d began to teach me about the need for prayer and intercession. Trust me, the East

Village was pretty run-down in those days and the streets were full of drug pushers and prostitutes and every New Age spirit going. So it was not long after a decent amount of trial and error that without the power of prayer, we knew we would be wasting our time. I have to say that this was probably one of the most powerful lessons that I learned in those early days—to touch Jewish ministry (that I was about to be led into) without prayer and intercession is like throwing out the baby with the bath water.

It was during this time that Richard invited a minister named Dick Simmons to visit One Accord and teach us about the power of prayer. Dick had a prayer ministry and was spending a lot of his time in the nation's capital to help with the prayer movement that was taking root there. There was also a movement going around the country at that time, calling the body to daily prayer. It was not long before we got caught up in it ourselves, opening the church at 5 AM to any and all who would join us in prayer. There were some powerful meetings when the Holy Spirit would meet us early in the morning and we would pray for New York, for the United States, and also for Israel and the Jewish people. The Holy Spirit would also lead us into warfare against certain spirits and principalities, especially against Islam, where the warfare was always the most intense.

Spiritual warfare happens in the heavenlies, which is obviously not in our dimension, but rather in a spiritual plain. While we are praying, our spirits get caught up with the Holy Spirit, and all of a sudden we can find ourselves in a battle, actually feeling the onslaught of good spiritual forces against bad ones. When praying in the Spirit in this manner, I can often feel a great surge with the enemy on the run and the spiritual plain being retaken for G-d—at least this is the best way I can describe it.

There was one meeting where the intercession and warfare was so intense that it actually thundered at the precipice moment of our prayers; we were all quite taken by it, but blessed at the same time. Not only did the presence of G-d flow in these meetings, but the prophetic was also regularly present, and it was here in these meetings that G-d began to deepen my burden for Israel. He also told me that I would be going into the Church to teach them about Israel, which was also confirmed to me on several occasions through a number of prophetic words. It was from Dick's meetings, who would pray with us every time he was in New York, that I started a prayer meeting for Israel, as I felt this burden increase within me.

I continued to oversee this prayer meeting for Israel for several years with another believer by the name of Diane Pearson and we learned a lot from the Holy Spirit. Diane was also English, and she had a special heart to pray for Israel. In these meetings, the Holy Spirit was always faithful to show up, He truly became our Teacher in the art of intercession as we cried out for Israel and warred against Islam in the heavenly realms. Not just to release the Jewish people, but also those caught under the grip of Islam. It was in these meetings that both Diane and I got well equipped for future prayer and intercession that He was about to lead us into for the Russian Jews in the 1990s.

That spring, One Accord had grown again; but at this time, Richard made a confession to the congregation and earnestly repented for not preaching the full counsel of G-d. From that point on, each Sunday for six months, Richard preached about the gifts of the Holy Spirit and how these gifts were for us today. He was determined to preach until the power of G-d fell in all of its fullness, and that is exactly what happened. We also met regularly for prayer, and once a month we had all-night prayer meetings, which I believe helped fuel the loosening of the Holy Spirit which came upon us.

In one of those all-night meetings with feathered pillow in hand, at about four o'clock in the morning, I prayed out a prayer. "Oh G-d, please send me a beautiful wife." Richard laughed and called an end to the meeting and we all went home. However, a few months earlier, he had prophesied to me that G-d was going to bring me a queen in the faith.

On one hot Sunday night in September, the power of the Holy Spirit fell on One Accord, and it was absolutely glorious, as if being in the very presence of G-d, known as the *Shekinah*, a Hebrew word for the glory and presence of G-d. Not only were many people healed, but demons were flying out of people and the presence of G-d truly started to set people free. I remember one Sunday when praying at the altar I started to pray for a woman in the neighborhood and as I was going to lay my hands on her, before I even touched her, her whole body jumped backward several feet and she fell onto the pews. Then she ran out of the church as quickly as she could. I later found out that she had been practicing witchcraft and was obviously not interested in stopping.

With Richard's leadership, his boldness, and a body of young disciples who were truly committed to the ministry, One Accord grew from ninety people to over four hundred in less than one year. We baptized many new believers and moved into a larger building on 3rd Ave and 7th Street to accommodate the growth, and the fullness of G-d continued to visit with us as our little ministry grew in strength. I was now totally focused on ministry at this point in my life and shared my faith with whoever would listen. G-d touched a number of lives through me, owing to the zeal of G-d that was in my heart and the willingness to share. However, it is also true to say that as I was learning to share my faith, I am sure I turned off a lot of people, including certain family members.

The Gospel is like a spiritual light in the darkness and there are many who just do not want to hear it; we need to learn how to be sensitive to those around us and show respect, which I was quickly learning, however this was not without error. It was during this time that Maxime Herman came to faith, she was the first Jewish person I helped to introduce to Yeshua. She was a friend and neighbor of Lucia Aloi, a feisty Italian believer who had grown up in the Roman Catholic Church and was a member of our group. Lucia had been sharing her faith with Maxime and invited her to the home group meeting that Lucia and I ran out of her apartment in Greenwich Village. Maxime was an attractive lady in her fifties and was divorced. Lucia asked me to spend some time with Maxime owing to our Jewish connection. She was quite taken by the passion and exuberance that I had for G-d and very quickly recognized the spiritual connection and was immediately drawn to find out more about Him. I started to meet weekly with Maxime around our home group meeting, and we would go through the Hebrew Scriptures together about Yeshua. Over a period of weeks, she started to believe that He was the Messiah and also became very excited about it as G-d began to open this door to her heart.

A number of weeks went by and despite her willingness to believe in Yeshua, she just could not accept the fact that He was actually G-d, and part of the triune revelation of G-d that Yeshua gave us with the New Covenant. No one was more familiar than myself with all of the barriers that both man and the devil had placed in front of any Jew now coming to the Messiah. I had painfully worked through them myself in my own return to G-d. And so one day, I turned to Maxime and asked her, "Do you believe that Yeshua was G-d and that He had come down to the earth in human form?" "I can't!" Maxime cried. "I just can't!" She was being tormented by this fact, and the devil would not let up on his grip of fear she was dealing with by taking this step of faith. However, Maxime was smart, and despite her now known resistance, she also recognized that it was really holding her back.

As discussed previously, Gentile believers must learn better to understand what we Jews actually have to go through because of all of the terrible things that have been done to our people in the name of Christ over the past two thousand years; as well as the additional inherent indoctrination not to accept Yeshua because we did not believe He was the Messiah. This is deeply entrenched in our blood, and every Jew who comes to faith always has to deal with this factor, which plays a major influence in all of our experiences in our return to G-d.

In reality, it wasn't so much that Maxime didn't believe that Yeshua was G-d, because inside she already knew. Instead, it was the horrible fear that the devil has placed around my people to prevent them from even getting to this place. After we discussed this, I led Maxime in a prayer to confess the fear she was experiencing and then in faith, which she said so beautifully as the tears were gushing down her face, "G-d of Israel, I love You, and Yeshua, I love You and accept that You are G-d." In reality, after Yeshua rose from the dead, fifty days later, He was the One to send the Spirit of G-d upon us to release the New Covenant. But how could He send the Spirit of G-d if He was not included in the G-dhead Himself?

In the New Covenant, we believe as all Jews do in one G-d as per the *Shema*, a beautiful Jewish prayer that many of us recite (see Deuteronomy 6:4-5). However, we also fully recognize the Spirit of G-d, the Fatherhood, whom we call Abba and now His beloved Son. One G-d, with three distinct roles uniquely intertwined into a *Elochim*, which is a Jewish word that actually already describes the plurality of G-d. Take a look at Genesis 1:26, which I have already addressed in an earlier chapter.

Immediately after Maxime said this prayer, she was supernaturally filled with the presence of G-d, but first she had to accept in faith that Yeshua was who His Word said He was. The wonder of the New Covenant is that when we yield our hearts in full surrender, in promise to G-d's Word in His actions, He fills us with His Holy Spirit, who actually represents both the Father and the Son. Then they come to live within our spirits to make us new. Without a doubt, it is a life-changing experience, and you will be forever changed.

G-d's presence was so strong between us that I was also weeping with tears of joy as I saw my new dear friend fully come to faith. It was a beautiful thing; and like me, Maxime joined One Accord and became like a sponge to her newfound faith, growing leaps and bounds. G-d regularly washed her soul and spirit with His love and cleansing hand.

When Jews finally return, many get on fire for G-d, because usually they have had to count the cost for their newfound faith. However, with Maxime, it was just a beautiful thing to see how quickly she grew in strength and intimacy with the L-rd, often teaching me a thing or two of her new findings in her own unique relationship with G-d.

G-d used me to help bring to faith a number of others, and I should mention a couple. Adrian Rolfs, a Brazilian model, was living in Pele's apartment while he was away (the famous soccer player) in the building where I lived, and she became on fire for G-d. And a delightful young lady from an African American background. Many of whom have gone on to experience their own deep spiritual walks with the L-rd.

Wherever I went, I shared Yeshua. I just could not contain the spiritual joy within my soul, and many others were touched as I would always invite them to our congregation or to the Models meetings, depending on what fit best. We also saw many men from the Bowery come to faith with major turnarounds in their lives, as well a number of models and actors from both fellowships.

In light of the power of G-d we were moving in, others were drawn to our ministry and we constantly shared our faith and ministered His love and His spirit to hundreds of people all around us. The now famous Messianic violinist, Maurice Sklar also visited One Accord, and we often helped him in his new spiritual journey with the L-rd. John DeLorean, the famous car maker, also came to faith during this time, and he visited our congregation with a friend who loved the L-rd.

Being drawn to evangelism, earlier that year I heard about a conference being held by Billy Graham for evangelists in Amsterdam. Billy Graham now had a vision to train and equip young evangelists from all over the world. The roster was full when I approached them; however, with a lot of prayer and persistence, they agreed to let me come, as long as I paid my own way, which I was perfectly prepared to do. The conference was held in July for ten days; and when I got there, I could not believe my eyes. In our first meeting, Billy Graham addressed the crowd of more than ten thousand evangelists from more than three hundred different countries. I was truly blessed. I had only been walking with G-d for about a year and a half, and here I was now being trained by one of the world's greatest evangelists. Hallelujah!

The Billy Graham organization, was quite a bit more conservative in faith than I was getting used to, however many of the young trainees were overflowing with His presence. There were a number of times in the conference when I could feel that the place was going to erupt in the Spirit, but then someone in the leadership would usually alert us and calm us down. I was bothered by this for a while, but here G-d began to teach me how He truly respects those in authority; and if He could bless it, why couldn't I? And soon after I got over my disappointment and tried to respect how others move in the Spirit of G-d.

There were some incredible speakers from all around the world, and for ten days, I was just floating in the Spirit. We were taught all aspects of evangelism: how to lay out messages and how to give responses. And they were especially focused on the follow-up of those who may have responded to our messages, as many would come. However, few would remain and become discipled, which a lot of attention was given to, to help new believers get grounded in the faith. Here I also met a few young believers from Israel who informed me of the young Messianic movement growing in the land, where there were approximately two thousand plus Jewish believers at the time. I also became friendly with an evangelist from Ghana, Reverend Nicholas Instiful, with whom I have stayed in touch for many years.

The Messianic movement was also growing in the United States, where an awakening had occurred in the late 1960s and early 1970s, right after Israel re-took Jerusalem in 1967. Not by coincidence, I believe, as soon as this happened, G-d started to reveal Himself once again to the Jewish people through belief in Yeshua, and the very young Messianic Movement had begun, with thousands of Jews coming to faith all across America.

In Ezekiel chapter 37, almost three thousand years earlier, it appears as if G-d took the young prophet out of time and showed him the dead bones of the Holocaust and that out of this death would come the new life of the nation of Israel. However, this prophecy appears to be in two main parts: the first was a physical awakening throughout the land, which happened in 1948; and the second where he talks about a spiritual awakening, which was just beginning to happen in our modern times. I have addressed this aspect in more detail in later chapters.

I only knew a little about the Messianic movement, which I was honestly not drawn to at this time. In my mind, its focus in those early years was too much on the religious aspects of Judaism and not enough on the presence of G-d, which often got a back seat as a result. To me, the forefront of the Jewishness of the New Covenant, was the intimacy that we had with the Holy Spirit where we would know His love and law on the inside of our hearts, as Yeshua has taught us that the Kingdom of G-d is from within (see Luke 17:21). For while our heritage was important, nothing should come before this. However, in defense of the Messianic movement, the Church had become so Gentile that there was just no place for Jewish believers to remain as Jews. As a result, later on I came into a much better understanding of this situation.

In fairness to Jewish believers, during these times, and still today, there are very few places a Jewish believer could go to in the Church that not only understood the call to the Jew but also fully supported their Jewish lifestyle, and this should not be the case. I was very fortunate to have met Maria and Richard Glickstein, who totally encouraged me to find the fullness of my faith as a Jew; and so as a result, I felt extremely secure that I had not converted to anything, but rather had returned to the G-d of my fathers. In addition, perhaps the extreme attachment to religious Jewish things during the infancy of the Messianic movement may have risen as a result of the Church's inaction toward them, as well as some of our own insecurities of now believing in a G-d who is presented to the world as Gentile even though He is totally Jewish.

I did, however, get to meet and spend time with Art Katz, a Jewish leader who had found the L-rd in the 1950s and who was filled with the Spirit of G-d. I was truly drawn to his ministry. I met Art in a prayer meeting at another one of those conferences that Richard and I were attending on the Holy Spirit and quickly became interested in his ministry. Art was also one of the first Jewish leaders in the Messianic movement and was truly focused on the power of G-d and all that He had to offer us.

For the most part, Art was ahead of his time for a very young and adolescent Messianic body, which was just beginning to find itself. Art believed in the re-gathering of the Jews back to the land and even set up his ministry home in Minnesota as a commune, which could be used later as a refuge location for Jews going back to Israel. Art also wrote a number of books; his testimony, *Ben Israel*, is a great read, especially for some of us who may be more intellectual in our approach. He also wrote about the Holocaust, as well as a number of prophetic books, which can be found on his Website, www.Benisrael.org.

One Accord was now booming, and our meetings were truly glorious with the worship filled with the presence and power of G-d. During the service, it was really difficult not to connect with the Spirit. In His presence, I would regularly listen for His voice into my life and the necessary direction that I may have been looking for as I was waiting on Him. Remember, my life now belonged to G-d, and I knew He had a perfect plan for me. And while it was up to me to seek Him for it, it was also up to Him to show and lead me in the right direction. Sometimes I pulled at Him like a spoiled child, but at least I was pulling, and I knew He took pleasure in that.

Chapter 11

DONNA COMES INTO MY LIFE

At this time, I began to seek the L-rd for future direction and did not want to go back into business. My mind and heart was set on becoming an evangelist, and I applied to Elim Bible College in upstate New York, where I wanted to get a more thorough and professional training. When the papers arrived, I was so excited and filled them out immediately. However, after I sent them off and for about a two-week period, the L-rd took away my peace. He gave me dreams almost every night to try to explain to me that it was not His will for me to go to Bible college; and to be honest, I really had a lot of difficulty letting go, as this is what I wanted to do with my life. Anyone who knows me will tell you that when I set my mind on something, I do not let go of it easily.

However after several days, I knew this was G-d speaking to me, and as a result I had to let it go so that my peace could return to my spirit. So I made a deal with the L-rd, if He was not going to let me go to Bible college, I asked him if I could learn through correspondence studies instead, and He agreed. So later that year, I put my apartment up for sale on 54th Street so I could reduce my expenses to study while I continued to help One Accord grow. During this time I met Donna, my future wife, praise G-d!

By this time, we were having the Bible studies at my apartment on Wednesday evenings. And on one particular night, I was walking my dog, Boo-Boo, before the meeting started. As I was waiting in the elevator to go back up to my apartment, in walks Donna. She was very pretty, but seemed quite pensive and nervous as we took our first elevator ride together up to my apartment, which was on the twenty-first floor. She explained to me that she was Jewish. I immediately replied in my still strong English accent, "Oh, I am Jewish too," which immediately broke the ice and the tension she was feeling. G-d had definitely planned that moment for us; and this opened the door for Donna to be more comfortable as a Jewish believer in the New Covenant.

Like me, Donna was also introduced to Yeshua through Gentile believers, a Catholic girl and a Protestant boy—young people who had already made their own connection with G-d and were now sharing their faith with others, and in this particular case, a nice Jewish girl from Queens, New York. Donna was earnestly seeking G-d for herself and was looking for answers from within, which current Judaism could not provide her. One day she walked into the Jews for Jesus office in New York City and was introduced to one of the leaders there, Baruch Goldstein. "If Jesus is the Messiah of the Jews and the King of Israel" she said, "I want to know Him." And right then and there she asked Him into her heart.

Donna then found out about One Accord, which was very close to where she lived in the East Village, and she visited the Bible study, which is where we met. Donna and I became friends, and she also joined the home group that Lucia and I were overseeing. By the time Donna came into my life, I was just beginning a healing process from a number of bad relationships, as well as some deeper relationship issues with my mother, most of which I was not even aware of at this time.

G-d was beginning to unravel my heart in this area, and I was just beginning to recognize my blindness in this place of my heart.

Little did I know at that time how G-d would use this relationship in my life to birth greater faith in me. G-d was about to start touching deeper and more sensitive places within me that I would not be so willing to share. This was quite painful to deal with and sometimes the deeper things of the faith, which truly bring about more of the depths of His character in our lives, really takes time to develop, almost like a fine bottle of wine.

You see, in the kingdom of G-d, He works in opposite ways to that of the world and it is actually through the weaknesses in our characters that He most often shines through us. However, with many of us, as He begins to work deeper into our hearts to bring about healing and cleansing, most of us actually resist. If you think of the heart for a moment like different rooms in a house, when He begins to knock on more sensitive doors, we usually do not allow Him in and rather keep the doors tightly closed. "No G-d, not this area!" And of course the Holy Spirit is so gentle with us; He is a perfect Gentleman, and He will not go anywhere within us without our agreement and invitation first.

Oh my, what a wonderful G-d! If only others in the world would know His love like this, they would definitely be less resistant to Him. *"He who began a good work in you will carry it on to completion until the day of Messiah Yeshua"* (Philippians 1:6). And *"My grace is sufficient for you, for my power is made perfect in weaknesses"* (2 Corinthians 12:9). The wonder of the New Covenant is when we truly yield our hearts and allow Him to flow through us in difficult places; it is here that we truly experience the wonder and power of the kingdom of G-d, as after death comes the resurrection—and the new life that without the former we could not experience the latter.

Many Messianic Jews understandably avoid the terminology of the cross, because that sign has been negatively used against us as

Jews. As a result, when around Jewish people we should always be sensitive to this fact, because it has become such a barrier between us in light of its use with all of the persecution against us. However, we should also never negate the power of the cross's mission in each of our lives, as it is so central to our faith. In our individual walks and deep within our hearts, this is where new life and healing stem from in the New Covenant The cross is representative of both death and new life in each of us, which is how G-d actually sets us free from within. In addition, please try to remember that the cross was a Jewish mission in the first place, ordained by the G-d of Abraham and willingly experienced by Yeshua, His Son, the Jewish Messiah, who was given first to the Jews before His word went out to the Gentiles.

While we may have certain sensitivities in our hearts stemming from where we used to be or operate from in our pasts, as each person's walk is different, if we keep yielding and keep trusting, we truly come into new areas of freedom in our lives, including healing. His grace not only frees us, but protects us too, as long as we continue to walk in obedience. This is the power of the New Covenant through Yeshua's mission, through the cross and the new life of the resurrection, for He has truly taken away our sins once and for all and delivers us spiritually from sin's curse of death into a new life in the Spirit of G-d. The issues that may have plagued or bound us in our past or were so strong once upon a time in our lives, now grow strangely dim. And the cross truly frees us from ourselves, as well as from the enemy's past grips on our lives. This is something that the world is truly always looking for, but keeps looking for it in all of the wrong places. Just like Yeshua said that the world did not know His peace because the peace of G-d can only come from His Spirit, so it is with healing and deliverance in each of our lives. True inner healing can only come from G-d by applying His principles and Word working from within us. That's why so many people in the world feel trapped by their own minds and emotions.

Except today, many are prescribed drugs to help them cope, but they never really find freedom and deliverance. Only by the power of G-d washing our minds and souls and delivering us unto faith through His Holy word, can every wall and barrier that exists within us be truly smashed. For the walls and obstacles I may have faced that seemed insurmountable to me before I met Yeshua have now either been completely removed or have been reduced, so they can no longer control me. For it is His truth combined with faith that operates deep within each of our souls to bring transformation and change (see Romans 12:1-2). All has been worked so marvelously by His Holy Spirit in a manner that is unique to each of us. It is also our weaknesses (see 1 Corinthians 12:9) that G-d will use to strengthen our faith as He initiates His healing and cleansing process over the course of our life experiences. This requires vulnerability and trust, yet both are needed to help Him open the door to greater healing and transformation in each of our lives.

This is what I truly loved about Richard Glickstein's teaching and emphasis on the faith. That we all have our own individual walks with G-d, and we are all to be freely led by the Holy Spirit, our guide, who will bring us into G-d's perfect will for each of our lives. What may be tempting for you could be completely normal for me and vice versa, which is why we always need to truly hold on to the great revelation of the New Covenant—that we actually know G-d for ourselves (see Jeremiah 31:34).

Therefore, we must also be lead individually by G-d Himself, which is why it is so important for each of us to know the voice of G-d in our own lives, as well as His Word. The Holy Spirit is truly our guide, and He will lead us and show us the way, as He directs. When you can really look at it like that, your life truly becomes an adventure and it takes on a whole new excitement, especially when you know that G-d is in the middle of it all. Hallelujah and praise the G-d of Israel!

It was January 1987 and in one of our Sunday meetings, Richard had a prophecy for me at the altar. However, it was not one of those that he whispered into my ear. No, instead, this was bellowed out to the whole congregation and everyone heard it, "By January 31st next year, you will know who you are supposed to marry!" Maybe Richard was fed up listening to all of my prayers (ha!), as I truly wanted to get married. However, there was no doubt that certain boldness came over him and we were all quite taken by his prophecy.

By this time, I had stopped dating but had also become more disciplined in this area of my life. There were still a number of women around me, mainly because of the Models ministry that I was still involved in. However, later that year, Yeshua led me to end my commitment there, but I stayed friends with most of the leaders in the group because they were also attending One Accord as well.

G-d was really beginning to focus more on this area in my heart and I knew it and wanted to be obedient to His direction. Donna and I were still just friends at this point, and I can remember being out with her and some other believers, when I actually shared the thought that if my wife was sitting right in front of me, I would not even recognize her. And there she was sitting right at the table, can you imagine? There was another incident that was somewhat similar to this that I would like to share.

At that time and for a number of years there had been a very popular Ukrainian restaurant on the corner of 2nd Avenue and 7th Street called Kiev. Great Ukrainian food at coffee shop prices, and many of us would eat there owing to our rather thin budgets. It was a Sunday afternoon and Richard had asked me to meet a new couple, Beau and Christine, who had just started coming to One Accord. They were both extremely gifted in the worship area, and would later take over the worship at One Accord.

As I was waiting for them outside, Donna walked into Kiev with two of our Jewish friends from One Accord, Carol and Allison Berkowitz, who were sisters, and they went to sit in the back of the restaurant. Donna and her friends started talking about marriage and husbands, and Donna said quite out of the blue in a joking manner, that the empty chair next to her had been reserved for her future husband. I had been waiting for Beau and Christine for well over half an hour and realized that they were not coming. No more than a couple of minutes after Donna had spoken those words, I went over and sat down in the very chair that Donna had pointed to! The girls were all laughing out loud as they could not believe what had just happened, but they wouldn't share with me what was said, telling me that it was a private joke.

G-d truly has a great sense of humor; in fact, I believe He created humor and loves to laugh with us! I think from that point Donna actually knew that we were to be married, as the L-rd had already told her. However, Mr. Spiritual, as I liked to think of myself in those days, was still quite blinded by this truth. During those next months, G-d began to whisper to me about Donna, but I was still not ready to hear Him.

By this time I had sold my apartment on 54th Street and was now sharing an apartment up town with one of my dear friends from One Accord. The rent was very affordable; and as a result, I only had to work part time while I was studying at Moody Bible College. There were many brothers at One Accord who were dealing with the homosexual lifestyle and trying to come out of it, which seemed and seems to be one of the greatest fights in modern Christianity. At One Accord we welcomed people from all walks of life. Their past background did not matter; it was moving forward that counted. And we looked at homosexuality just like any other sin and tried to win all the souls around us with the love of Yeshua, which gave us all the power to conquer and overcome our weaknesses.

During this time, my other cosmetic project had come to an end, and I started working as a waiter at Maxim's, the famous Parisian restaurant on Madison Avenue, now owned by Pierre Cardin. Remember at the beginning of my walk I had said to G-d that I did not care if I swept streets or waited on tables? I was now moving in this direction, as I looked to finance myself while studying. I quickly learned that any honest day's work was respectable, even though my family was quite taken by it. I really loved serving people and took full advantage of my English accent and played the butler, which Americans really loved. One of my friends, Nick De Marco, who Maria had also brought to faith, was the president of the Pierre Cardin Company in the U.S., and he helped me get the job at the restaurant, where I stayed for a year and a half while I was studying.

It was on a One Accord camping trip that Donna and I first felt things for each other and it was quite romantic at that. Around a warm, bustling fireplace in the middle of the woods on a cool summer's night, our romance began as we shared our first kiss. It was all quite innocent, almost as if G-d had wiped away my promiscuous past.

Donna and I continued to date over the summer, and I took a part-time job running a telephone drive for a young man named Pastor Willie who was organizing a spiritual outreach and parade in New York's Central Park called Jesus Loves New York. The event took place at the beginning of September and drew many church groups from all over the city, with many of their leaders sharing a few words from the platform between the musical performances. I had worked hard to help Willie make this outreach a success, and we actually led thousands of people in a parade down Central Park West and into the park for the performance.

It was a very exciting day, and the L-rd was glorified through it. While I was standing on the platform, the Holy Spirit fell on me and I began to weep as His love and presence touched my spirit and soul and He spoke these words, "You are going to have a son, and you are to give him the name Joshua." I was so excited and went to share the word with Donna who was also at the event. She already knew because G-d had already told her previously. Please keep in mind that we were only dating and had not yet discussed marriage.

At the last couple of Wimber conferences that we attended, Richard had developed a relationship with a man by the name of Bob Jones, who was a prophet of the L-rd. It was during this time in the body of Messiah that G-d was beginning to reestablish the five-fold ministries of the faith that Rabbi Paul spoke of in his letter to the Ephesians (see Ephesians 4:11), and Bob Jones was definitely gifted in the prophetic area. When he ministered, he would tell people things that only the person or G-d actually knew about themselves. So Richard invited him to come and minister in New York—we were all very excited about his visit.

Aside from ministering at the congregation, we set up two additional meetings. One for the leaders of One Accord, which was held at the apartment I was sharing and another at Blanca Pappas's apartment, who was Donna's close friend, for some of the others in the church who were interested in a one-on-one session with the prophet.

I have never forgotten the words that Bob Jones prophesied to me and neither has Donna. He told me that I was going to be an evangelist to the nations; but beforehand, G-d would be removing a couple of leeches that were still part of me and that required inner healing. He told Donna that she was going to be a prophetess, someone in the spirit in the New Covenant who can see things, visions as well as the future, as the Holy Spirit leads in this gifting.

He also foretold both Richard and me of our work to the Russian Jews, which at the time did not make any sense to either of us. We were not aware then of what was about to happen with the former Soviet Union, but we knew that G-d knows the beginning from the end. I then released these words back to the Father, as He had begun to teach me to do when it came to the future and prophetic words that may come to us. Otherwise they can be confusing when we try to fit them into the puzzle for ourselves instead of using them as encouragement and future guidance, which is why these words are given to us in the first place.

In light of my past, our courtship was somewhat erratic. G-d was beginning to touch and heal a lot of my fears and insecurities, but I often resisted in the process because it did not feel right. This is why we can't always go by our feelings, because often if our lives are off in a certain area, so are the feelings that are usually attached to them. However, G-d quickly showed me that these feelings were not part of His Spirit, but rather part of my old nature that He was beginning to change and transform. He greatly encouraged me to work through them and allow the Word of G-d and my faith in Him to wash them away, which was no easy process for me. However, I knew this was correct, just as I begun to see how blinded I had become in this area of my heart.

I knew I had to yield this place within me to Him and allow His strength to work through me, which was very challenging and required a great deal of trust. In this place I had no strength of my own and needed to be completely dependent on Him, which caused a greater brokenness within me. I was falling in love with Donna, but the wounds of my past fought hard and this became a battle I knew I had to win—rather, it was a battle He had to win within me. For the first time in my new relationship with G-d, I was meeting strongholds from my past that did not want to let go and that I did not have the strength to overcome myself even though I knew they were not right anymore.

I did not share any of this with Donna at the time, as I did not think it was appropriate, but she was also very patient with me. I knew by now that Donna was to be my wife, as He kept telling me. As a result, despite my struggles, I knew Him well enough by now that overcoming some of my patterns and weaknesses from my past was His will for me and that He would give me the strength to overcome them. This is indeed exactly what happened as I began to trust Him more with these deeper areas in my heart and allow His healing to come in. On January 31, 1988, on a beach in the Hamptons close to my mother's home on Long island, I bent my knee and proposed marriage to Donna. It was a beautiful sunny day and unusually warm for January.

Richard's prophecy had been correct and from that point to the beginning of our marriage, we had a much more peaceful time truly developing our love for one another and beginning to make plans with our families. A few weeks later, I planned the giving of the engagement ring by placing three dozen red roses up the stairs of my apartment on 93rd Street, right into my living room where I had circled the ring with more flowers. The plan was interrupted when we were led to minister to a person in our building. Then a word came to us from the L-rd that our lives would often be interrupted because of His ministry to others around us.

In reflection of those times in my life, I wish I had sought additional counseling, as there were obviously deep wounds in my life from my past that I needed to continue to work on, some of which I ended up bringing into our marriage. However, it was not long after we were married that my cries for deliverance were answered and G-d gave me a new and fresh heart full of love for my wife. What an amazing G-d we serve, who truly loves us as a doting Father, if we can only learn to trust His will for our lives, which sometimes can be quite challenging. However, what discipline ever feels good at the time, yet in the end reaps the right fruit and harvest, because the L-rd develops those whom He loves (see Hebrews 12:5-6).

My cousin and friend, Brian Davies, also lived in New York; he retired very early in life as he had become very successful in the London real estate market, where his company was bought out. Brian was single and gay, and he was about fifteen or so years older than me. He was especially interested in my faith and without doubt was being drawn to me in this stage of his life. Owing to his lifestyle as well as his Jewish background, he had a lot of resistance to my faith—yet at the same time, he always wanted to hear about it, constantly asking me questions. I had no problem with any of this and owing to my calling back to my people, resistance just came with the territory. In addition, One Accord was full of people from a gay background who wanted to walk with G-d, although I was beginning to recognize for sure the incredible grip that this spirit had on men and women who opened themselves to this lifestyle, either through their bloodline, or by choice.

I did not know if Brian had already contracted AIDS before we met and became friendly, however, after a year or so, he told me about it, as he was beginning to show the horrible signs of this disease all over his body. We continued to meet, and he continued with his numerous questions, honestly learning a lot about the faith and absorbing everything I was sharing with him. But whenever it came to a discussion about prayer and acceptance, he quickly refused and this door quickly ended our discussion. However, I could tell deep down that he was in great need, yet his lifestyle would just not let go and this prevented him from getting any further with the L-rd. With Brian, none of the Jewish resistance stuff seemed to matter. He apparently already had a deeper understanding of spirituality, and he knew there was something special about Yeshua. As much as he seemed to want to believe, he could just not go there, and like I used to do, he laughed his way out.

Three months later, Brian was on his death bed in one of the larger hospitals in New York where I had already visited him a number of times. I personally witnessed firsthand how quickly AIDS robbed and stripped away Brian's life; just as it had from a number of other men at One Accord, who I also had become friendly with; it was just awful. By now, he could not speak, and on this particular visit, which was to be our last, I noticed he was crying. With great difficulty and a lot of time, he scribbled down his thoughts on a scrap piece of paper. This is what he wrote, "I am ready to accept Yeshua now; can you please pray for me?"

My heart broke and right there and then, and I led Brian in a prayer to accept Yeshua into his heart, to confess his sins and ask for G-d's Spirit into his heart. It was one of those sovereign moments in my life—my first family member to accept the L-rd, and I know one day I will see Brian again in heaven.

My mother still had her cosmetic company at this time, and she had experienced some considerable success. She wrote a book on makeup that she promoted across the United States and was even one of Oprah's first interviews. Sometimes my mother was overpowering, and she hated the fact that Yeshua was in my life but was learning to cope with it in her own way. However, she was dead set against Donna and I marrying in Yeshua's name. But Donna's father, G-d bless his soul, chose to respect our wishes, and since he and Donna's mum were paying for the wedding, my mother did not have that much say in the matter.

Chapter 12

A NEW BEGINNING, A NEW DIRECTION

It was 1988 and still quite rare and unusual for Jewish people to believe in Yeshua, as the Messianic movement and awakening had only just arrived several years ago in the late '60s and early '70s. It was like a sin for a Jewish person to believe in Jesus, and this was not an easy period with our families. But it also presented many opportunities for us to share our faith, and neither Donna nor I ever had a problem with that. On the contrary, we were always looking for opportunities to explain the most wonderful love of G-d that we actually felt from Yeshua in the New Covenant.

Donna and I stayed faithful to G-d to our wedding day, which goes so contrary to how people live and operate in this modern day, but we both knew G-d's Word and were determined to stay obedient to it. June 14 came around quickly, and Donna's parents gave us a beautiful wedding at the Water's Edge Restaurant in Long Island City. We asked Richard Glickstein to marry us and handle the ceremony, despite my mother's objections.

We had a beautiful *Chuppah* made, which is a special canopy that all Jewish people are married under. The atmosphere was intense to say the least, as nearly all of our family guests were Jewish. And no doubt, this was most probably all of their first experiences of two Jewish people getting married in Yeshua's name. We could have cut the atmosphere with a knife, especially every time Richard mentioned Yeshua's name in the ceremony. Under the Chuppah my mother cringed and my father-in-law groaned, "Oy! Oy! Oy!" What a scene for a movie!

Richard received a word for us right under the Chuppah, which he shared with us privately: in light of our calling to our people, we would often experience this type of burden and tension and that sometimes it would be difficult, but that His grace was sufficient for us, amen. Despite the pressure, the ceremony was beautiful with some of our friends from One Accord singing songs and making toasts. It was a beautiful day and an amazing wedding, and the L-rd truly released a spirit of joy into the party, as everyone had a fantastic time and we were all blessed. Donna and I were finally married, and we could not believe it! Hallelujah, praise G-d!

Both Donna and I are strong-willed individuals and as much as we loved each other, marriage was definitely an adjustment for us in our first couple of years, as it is for so many people, learning to live with another. However, we always seemed to muddle through, as He was always at the center of our relationship and we both pulled on His strength and love when we disagreed. And so often those silly little issues would just melt away; but make no mistake about it, Yeshua was definitely our anchor, and anyone who was around us always knew it.

I continued to work at Maxim's for several months after our wedding, but was now sensing the call to provide a better living for my new family. We purchased a one bedroom apartment on 24th Street, between 2nd and 3rd Avenues. As a result, I leaned on my old cosmetic contacts and went after the president of Del Labs, Dan Wassong, looking for a job, which I eventually got. However, I entered the company at a low management level and ended up working for a vice president who was obviously quite intimidated by my creativity. She literally cornered me until I decided to leave the company.

One day in prayer about my future, the L-rd gave me a clear word from the book of Nehemiah (chapter 1), to go back and rebuild the walls of my mother's business, which was now struggling. My mother wanted me to come back and help her in the business, which I was quite reluctant to do owing to past experiences, until I got the word from the L-rd, and then knew it was it His will. My stepfather was still not an easy person to get on with, on top of which he now suffered from bladder cancer, which made it even harder, as he was often in pain and was quite grumpy as a result. However, I knew G-d had character lessons for me here in trying to love and get on with my stepfather during this time. Not only was he very tough, but he was often mean, which I attributed to childhood issues that he never dealt with in his own heart. I really tried my best to love him and to be as patient as possible, but he certainly did not make it easy for me.

Sometimes G-d puts people in our lives who are definitely not easy to love and who can make things very difficult for us. However, in these types of cases, as believers, it is His divine strength that He wants us to not only call upon, but be dependent on at the same time. As a young man, this was definitely a new trial for me in my character, which I did not often pass. However, I never gave up on him and continued to persevere, confessing and repenting and trying to get back on the path whenever I got into my own will by reacting to the circumstances. Trials are never easy at the time, but G-d definitely uses them to both shape and mold our characters.

When I got back into my mother's business, it was far weaker than I had first thought and they were very close to going out of business, with barely enough cash flow to keep the business afloat. They were having difficulty trying to support their current business model, as it required a lot of financial support on the promotional and marketing side, which they could now no longer afford. In addition, there was certainly no additional investment capital to help turn the business around. All I had was a lot of discontinued merchandise, and with G-d's help and guidance and a lot of prayer, I used these old goods to reestablish my mother's brand into the mass market. I sold them at lower price points than her products were usually sold for in department stores, as this market was almost completely dried up by this point.

I also began to develop some new product and merchandising concepts for the company with the cash we generated from the old inventory and the new marketplace responded very well to them. Within a short period of time, we opened up hundreds of new outlets for the brand, and we began to turn around the sales of the company. However, cash flow was still very tight; and, as a result, a couple of years later, I moved away from the company as a full-time employee and continued to manage the brand on a commission basis so I could take on other products to represent and sell, while still helping my mother's company grow.

That spring we visited England to spend some time with my father in Wells, near Bath. A year earlier I had received a word from the Holy Spirit that there was a curse upon my family, but I did not know what that meant. I found this strange in the beginning but this word would not depart from my spirit; and after a while, as a result I sought spiritual counsel about it from Richard. Not only had Craig, my brother, and I experienced the sting of this curse with the loss of two of our businesses, but there was also a string of bankruptcies on both sides of my immediate family, including the businesses of my father, my grandparents, and Uncle Stephen.

After an in-depth prayer and counseling session with Richard, he confirmed this word to me. However, he said that this curse would need to be broken by my father who was the head of my family, and I got the sense that this needed to happen, in order for me and my family to get on with our lives. I did not know who had placed the curse upon us, but thought that someone in my family may know, so I started to inquire. After bringing this to my father's attention, he immediately responded that one of his aunts had cursed him when he took over the family furniture business in England, after buying them out. However, despite his acknowledgment of this, when I asked him if we could pray about it, he somewhat laughed it off at the time, so we could not really properly address it.

However, the next year before we visited my father in England, the L-rd told me that the time had come for this curse to be broken and that He would take care of it. Sounds strange I know, as things in the spirit can often be, but this is exactly what happened. We spent a week or so in England, as I wanted to show Donna where I had grown up, and several days with my father, who gave us a really nice holiday. During our last night in Bath, we were having dinner, and right there at the table I prayed silently to the L-rd about addressing the curse, as I did not want to bring it up until the right time and get another negative response to moving on this.

Please know that my father was still lovingly trying to understand everything that had happened to me, and I knew this had affected his response. No more than a few seconds after I had asked the L-rd to raise the issue, my dad turns to me and says, "Son," which he usually called me, "do you remember that curse you brought up to me last year about the old family business?"

"Yes Dad," I replied.

"Well, I have been thinking about this, and I agree with you. I think we need to break it."

Donna and I could not believe what we were hearing, and I immediately responded by sharing with Dad some of the things I had learned about this and how we should proceed. I explained to him that as the patriarch of the family, we needed to pray together and break the curse. He would have to exert his authority as the head of the family, so we agreed to meet the following morning at the hotel and pray together.

It was a beautiful English summer day and the sun was shining brightly. May was always my favorite month in England for weather, as the rest of the summer can sometimes be so dreary. We met in the back garden of an old country mansion and there we joined hands in prayer. Aside from reading from certain Jewish prayer books, this was the first time I had prayed with my father; both Donna and I were very much touched in our hearts, as he prayed so eloquently to G-d. I raised the issue in prayer and then Dad agreed. It was not only a beautiful prayer time, but something very strategic was broken that day that was to change my family's business lives and allow us to prosper again as we broke this curse.

Curses can be real, as seen from the Scriptures, but we do not need to go searching for these things; if they are there, G-d will make them known. However, when people ignore these signs and warnings, the power of curses can have their effects on many lives.

Chapter 13

LORD & BERRY IS BORN

It was during this time that I definitely felt the L-rd drawing me back to business. However, as a young man, I had already carried a lot of responsibility. In Pirate cosmetics, which I had built with my brother before I met the L-rd, I really felt the burden of business responsibilities upon my shoulders. And to be perfectly honest, I did not want to go back to running my own company; if that was what it was like, I did not want it at all. However, when we earnestly try to live out our walks with Messiah in obedience, we have to be willing to go places that we personally might not want to tread, and this was now the case with me. G-d's burden is light and His yoke is easy (see Matthew 11:20), but I had not yet experienced this in my business life, so the latter was all I knew and as a result I was fearful of it and was definitely quite pensive.

The Holy Spirit is extremely gentle and loving with us as I have already mentioned, especially with areas that He knows are sensitive and delicate. He lovingly pulls at our heart and speaks His will through many means aside from His still quiet voice that lives within us, as well as the Word of G-d. He also uses people and circumstances, and if we want His perfect will for our lives, we must be willing to look at all of these indicators and allow Him to piece them together for us as we seek Him for direction in our lives. Remember, my life now belonged to Him, so I never wanted to move ahead without His direction, in order that His peace would continue to flow and that my decisions and choices would be in the light.

As a result, it was on a large sand dune on the beach in Southampton, New York, while in the midst of prayer that I became conscious of resisting Him in this area. Right there and then, I finally gave in to His new will and direction for my life, which was to form a new company and start a new brand. However, this time I was also conscious of the financial burden that may lay ahead of me because of my past experience and so in need of His partnership, that I decided to name Him first in this new venture and called the company Lord & Berry. Whatever I did, I wanted Him to be with me in the midst of it all.

I can honestly say that in the seven years that I owned and managed this company, it was not up until the very last few days that I ever experienced fear again or worry or nervousness. He truly carried this burden for me, as I continued to release it back to Him. Little did I even expect or anticipate in this next phase of my business life, both the natural and spiritual plans that He had in store for me in this company and the journey I was about to embark upon. He was about to mushroom this little company into the limelight, literally from nothing and almost overnight.

I did not have the funds to start a new brand, which required investment. But shortly after I made this decision to move ahead, my father approached me without knowing any of my experience, asking if I was in need of any help to get some kind of a venture going. I immediately told him that I needed $25,000 and that I would pay him back as soon as I could. My father had always been there for me in my life, and while initially he had trouble understanding my newfound faith, he never stopped trying to help me get my life on the right path, which I was extremely grateful for, as I did not expect this from him at this point in my life.

I developed a creative relationship with Nick Puccia, a free-lance graphic designer, who helped me with all of the artwork and subsequently became my art director. We have worked very closely together over the years and he has become one of my dearest friends. In the beginning, I focused on the eye area, so I developed a new concept with eyeliners as well as a new trademark, Dramateyes. This new concept focused more on function than colors, as my budget was also limited and black eyeliners always outsold colors quite dramatically. I also merchandised it in a very unique display capitalizing on all of the design work that I had learned in my father's furniture business. Because the opening order was so small on new products, many accounts looked to take it on, and the products sold really well. Within six months, Lord & Berry was now being sold in more than four hundred accounts in the New York market as well as throughout the beauty supply market nationwide, which I had sold in my Pirate days.

Shortly after this initial success, my stepfather became very distrusting of me, so I could no longer run and manage both brands. As a result, I left my mother's company, which I had wanted to continue to manage because they needed my help. I now focused on my own business, continuing to sell and represent other products to help pay the bills. Here I was again back at the helm of my own company, but was also in need of additional income. Donna worked as a sales representative for a temporary employment agency and aside from the additional brands that I repped, I also worked catering jobs at night to help cover the bills. When I look back on those days, I often wonder how we ever managed to get by—but we give thanks to G-d, who always takes care of all of our needs and is truly our provider, Jehovah Jirah.

I would go out during the day and pound the pavements calling on all of our accounts in the Metro New York area and Philly markets, often putting holes on the soles of my shoes with all of my walking.

At night when I returned home, I would enter all of the orders into the computer and then walk them down to the garage attendant, Rod Arango, who stored all my products in his living room in his Brooklyn home and who handled all of my shipping. You cannot replace hard work, but it certainly helps to have G-d on your side.

Donna and I continued to fellowship at One Accord, and our ministry definitely moved more in a Jewish direction. We began to hold Passover Seders for the group, further educating the congregation on their Jewish roots and heritage. On weekends in the summer, we would go up to the Catskill mountains and stay with Donna's parents, where on almost every occasion, we would end up sharing our Jewish faith about Yeshua with my in-laws' friends, some of whom were Holocaust survivors.

Donna's father had just turned sixty, and he suffered from diabetes and soon after contracted lung cancer. My father-in-law had a great sense of humor and he was the one who would usually open up the door of conversation for us. "Why don't you tell them about Jesus?" he would say in one of his joking voices. However, it was really him whose heart was honestly seeking and searching and who wanted help with all of his suffering and the pain he was feeling inside. Not just his physical pain, but the emotional pain he had from his childhood. By now he had already seen and began to witness the good things that were happening in his daughter's life because of Yeshua, which neither of Donna's parents could deny.

The next couple of years, both Donna and I began to adjust to married life; and, while I continued with prayer and intercession for Israel and my ministry at the Bowery, it was a quieter time for us both, focusing more now on our careers. Except our Passover outreach was growing and that next spring we sat over seventy people at our Seder at One Accord. Before we married, Donna had rented an apartment in the East Village on 2nd Avenue and 10th Street right opposite Saint Mark's church. Since my lease on 92nd Street was up, I moved into Donna's apartment, which was a bit of a culture shock for me at that time. Despite One Accord's outreach, it was still different when you were living right in the midst of some strange and wild spirits that the East Village seemed to be famous for in those days, and it wasn't exactly the safest neighborhood either. When walking Boo-Boo in the neighborhood, I would often get into some good street conversations with both drug pushers and prostitutes on my evening walks around the block.

It was during this time that G-d really began to make His calling for us back to our people much clearer. After all, we were naturally surrounded by Jewish people through our family and friends. Through lots of trial and error, we were eager to engage the people around us in conversations about G-d, and this period of our lives became a great learning ground for us in further developing a Jewish ministry.

On one occasion on a Sunday night, Donna and I were having dinner at 2nd Avenue Deli, a famous old Jewish delicatessen in the East Village, which was very popular with the Jewish community. While we were eating, the Holy Spirit spoke to me and told me to get up and tell them about Yeshua. I was immediately very nervous as I looked around me, as I did not think that there was one Gentile in the whole place. However, I knew the L-rd had spoken to me, and as a result, I had to be obedient. Maybe I had just reread in Ezekiel where G-d had told him to speak to the people and if he didn't that G-d would hold him accountable for it. For while I knew in the New Covenant we had His grace when we did not respond correctly, I knew I had to speak and could feel His presence welling up inside me.

I stood up and out came these words, "To my fellow Jewish friends of New York City, I am an English Jew from London, and in this great city of yours, I have come to find that Yeshua, Jesus, is the

Jewish Messiah." Immediately, as soon as I mentioned the very name of Jesus, almost every man in the place got up and started screaming at me. I could not believe what was happening; many were enraged and started to shout me down until I stopped. For a moment, we thought they might get violent, but after I sat down, the noise subsided and everyone went back to their meals.

As we left the restaurant, we were trying to understand why the L-rd had asked me to speak to them. And as we were walking down 2nd Avenue, we noticed one family leaving at the same time who seemed to have a very different response to us than the rest of the people. We never spoke to them, but had the sense that my actions and words may have been for them. Sometimes we never know how and what we do will actually impact others. However, I was quickly reminded firsthand of the deep-rooted anger toward Yeshua that was embedded in the hearts of my people from all of the anti-Semitism that had taken place, mostly in the name of Christ. And while I completely understood where they were coming from, my heart was also grieved. Yet a calm reality set in as to what may lie ahead for us to win our people back to faith and that it was never going to be easy.

For Donna and I, we never felt more Jewish after Yeshua came into our lives, but I began to recognize the great divide between my people and belief in Yeshua. And now felt a greater need to be able to properly explain all of this in a way that my people could understand it. The New Covenant was a fulfillment of all of the Hebrew Scriptures that foretold of the Messiah's coming and Yeshua fulfilled each and every one of them.

To me, when the G-d of Abraham circumcised my heart with His Holy Spirit that day on my bedroom floor, I did not convert to a foreign faith, but as a Jew, I actually returned to my own. Jews do not convert, they return to what was already given to them, even though we have become separate from it. Remember, Yeshua came first to the House of Israel so that the New Covenant would be given to us first, to fulfill G-d's Word and His ordained order in His spiritual family, to the Jew first and then the Gentile (see Romans 1:16). Gentiles convert to what was already established as a Jewish faith; and indeed when Gentiles believe in Yeshua, they become adopted children of Abraham, and like us inherit the same covenants given to Israel through Isaac, the child of a promise.

For even as I felt their hostility toward me for crossing this line, I also understood their anger and their pain, and it caused me to want to love them even more and win them over to faith in a loving G-d who laid down His life for them, just as He had done for the whole world.

Maybe that experience in the deli was actually for Donna and me, so we could see the reality and scope of the mission field He had called us to, and the deep chasms between the faiths of the Old and New Covenants. Whatever the reason was, it was definitely an eye-opener for us both. I knew I needed to learn to better to articulate what I believed to help my Jewish friends and family understand the whole picture.

Chapter 14

LIFE AND DEATH

That next summer, Donna conceived, and while we may not have been prepared financially for a baby, as we had just begun to focus on our careers, we were very happy and full of faith. We purchased an apartment on 23rd Street between 2nd and 3rd Avenues. A couple of years earlier we had the word from the L-rd about our son Joshua being born, and surely enough on March 25, 1990, Joshua Leo Berry was born. Leo means lion and his Jewish name was Lemmel, after his grandfather on Donna's side, which means lamb. Very appropriate for the month of March, which comes in like a lion and goes out like a lamb. In alignment with the covenants and the Word of G-d, on the eighth day, Joshua was circumcised. I could not remember my Jewish name from my Barmitzvah, so the moil who performed the ceremony renamed me Gedalliah, which means G-d is great. The next month, we dedicated Joshua's life to the L-rd at One Accord and a prophetic word came forth that G-d was also calling his life to his people and would use him accordingly.

I was now very much focused on my family and getting my business off the ground. Building any type of business is always hard work. In the beginning while its foundations are being built, there is rarely any extra time to be had or enjoyed. I can often remember how dry it felt, the long hours as well as the moonlighting to help pay our bills, but we do in life what is necessary. I knew and had the hope in my heart that I was building our future and enjoyed my work, while still continuing to share my faith with whoever would listen.

Donna had a cousin who had been quite successful in the financial markets, and one day when we were spending some time together, he asked me what I was doing for a living. I told him about our new business, and after I explained it to him, he asked me, "How can you make a living off five black eyeliners?" His question was both realistic and practical, but he had no idea what G-d was about to do with this little business and how it was about to be multiplied. I was so focused on running the day to day of my business, I had not given this a lot of thought, but I knew if I could create a demand and build a decent distribution for it, consumers would start asking for more. And this is exactly what happened.

In the next year, we expanded those five black eyeliners into a whole group of eyeliner products with lots of great and exciting colors that also began to sell very well. That next year, I dropped all of the other brands I was representing and dedicated all of my time to building the Lord & Berry brand, which was really beginning to grow.

During this time my father-in-law's sickness increased, and Donna began to spend more time with him. He had been a hard-working man and held a couple of jobs most of his career as a mail carrier for the post office, as well as working other jobs on the side to boost their income. He had just retired and was eagerly looking forward to it when he took a turn for the worst and contracted lung cancer on top of his diabetes.

He was very drawn to Donna, and with her newfound love and relationship with G-d, she was able to reach out to him with love and compassion. This time was greatly beneficial to both of them, as he had not been the greatest communicator as a parent and they had grown apart during her early adolescent life. He was really hurting physically, but he was also searching for inner relief. As he got worse, he found great solace and relief in what Donna was sharing; she began to open up the Word of G-d to him. He became like a sponge and would soak up whatever Donna would share with him. This went on for several months, and during this time we were earnestly praying that he would awaken to Yeshua. He also continued to open the door for us to speak to all of his friends and by now, most of them knew that belief in Yeshua wasn't so Gentile after all. We were not only sharing our faith in a Jewish context, but we were living it too and they could feel our love for them, which helped them to at least listen better to what we had to say.

One September weekend we visited Donna's parents in the Catskills. It may have been on Rosh Hashanah, the Jewish New Year, which sometimes comes earlier in September. It was later at night and we were sitting and talking in their living room when Artie cried out in desperation. It had all been too much for him, and the pain he was suffering, as well as the blindness that had recently come upon him, was too much to bear. He just broke down.

Suddenly the presence of G-d arrived in the room and we could feel His love as thick as the air that was enveloping us, and we all began to weep. We cannot see the Spirit of G-d, He is like a wind that comes and goes; however, when He comes, you know it and can feel His presence. You can immediately see how He effects all around Him, whether bringing us into His peace or causing us to become uncomfortable because of our own sins or weaknesses, which may not have been dealt with yet.

Artie, Donna, and I and even Gertie, Donna's mother, who was still very skeptical toward our faith, started weeping. In that moment we asked Donna's father to open his heart to the L-rd, which he did willingly and without any resistance. He asked Yeshua to come into his heart, and he gave his life over to Him in faith. It was one of those incredible moments that we never want to forget in life. The G-d of heaven and earth loved Artie so much that He came to visit him with His love and His peace, and all of us could feel His presence in the room as Donna's father came to faith. Three months later, Artie passed away. We both knew and had the comfort that he was truly being set free of his pain and suffering and moving on into a heavenly place where he would be free. While we felt sad to lose him, we also felt relief for him from his suffering as we mourned his loss.

One Accord had really grown by now, even with the Wilkerson brothers arriving in New York City and establishing a major congregation right in the heart of Times Square. It did eventually have an effect on us. David and Don Wilkerson were prominent leaders in the body of Messiah and were very well-known for their evangelistic work to gangs and drug addicts. In the early 1960s, David Wilkerson was guided by the Holy Spirit to come to New York City and he led a former gang member, Nicky Cruz, to the L-rd and the media was all over it. He also wrote a book about it, which has become a classic, *The Cross and the Switchblade*, which has sold over fifteen million copies worldwide. From this they built and established a fantastic work for the L-rd called Teen Challenge, helping both drug addicts and alcoholics get free from addiction and back into productive life. Teen Challenge now has more than one thousand centers in eighty-seven countries worldwide.[1]

In the late 1980s David and Don Wilkerson started having revival meetings in Times Square, and the L-rd called them to plant a congregation, which is still thriving today right in the middle of Times Square, with thousands of members.

We were not envious of this new work as it was also an answer to many of the prayers and intercession that Dick Simmons and others had led us in to help birth this work in the Spirit. We were both pleased and excited to have been able to contribute somehow to this great new effort. And we were grateful that such a large spiritual organization was taking note and giving more attention to New York City, which was and is so desperate for the message of Yeshua. Unfortunately, the next year, 1990, Richard Glickstein and his wife, Maria, separated and eventually divorced. It was a major blow to all of us at One Accord and especially to Richard and Maria and their family.

In those five or six years, Richard had achieved some amazing things in our little group, and many young believers like me were truly grounded and strengthened in the faith. I will always be truly grateful for those founding years in my faith, which helped shape me for my future work in the kingdom of G-d.

One Accord did not break up, but Richard brought in new leaders, Mark and Colleen Handy, who had been previously ministering in India. We did not feel led to stay at this point, and in fact actually felt released from our connection there. We were being led to visit the new congregation in Times Square. We had been at many of the opening meetings that the Wilkerson's held back in 1989, which were just terrific and full of G-d's presence. That previous year we had also visited, as they had brought in a new preacher from Israel named Reuven Doron. He had great teachings on Israel and the Church, all of which I thoroughly agreed with and was greatly blessed to hear from this pulpit, and later we brought Reuven Doron to One Accord to speak.

As G-d closes doors, it is not usually long before new ones open and this was definitely the case for Donna and I as we moved our spiritual home to Times Square Congregation. We had made some everlasting relationships with many of the founding members of One Accord, whom we will never forget. We had worked together and seen G-d move mightily in our presence on numerous occasions and shared some wonderful memories. A few of these special friends include: Phil and Joya Prestamo, Cathy and Richard Cain, Rex and Joy Duval, Jeff and Laura Calenberg, Nick and Anni Demarco, Jon Wright, Bob Wallis, Darien Jaynes, Goerge Cabral, Bill and Dawn

Ruff, Beau and Christine Stroupe, Blanca Pappas, Richard Davis, John Vigario, Patrick Fortemps, Lucia Aloi, Dominic and Leslie Crincoli, Rowland and Bernice Bestwina, Ron Gitelman, and many others—too many to mention.

ENDNOTE

1. http://www.globaltc.org; accessed April 23, 2012.

Chapter 15

JEWISH MINISTRY AT TIMES SQUARE AND THE BUSINESS BOOMS

Over those past couple of years, I had developed a new friendship with another Jewish believer named Arnie Klein. Arnie and Joannie had visited One Accord occasionally, and he was working for the New York Bible Society at that time. He was also one of the leaders of the Jewish ministry at Times Square with another friend, Chuck Cohen. Arnie encouraged me to join their efforts. Times Square had amazing Bible and spiritual teachings from the pulpit, and we were all built up in the Spirit.

From David and Don Wilkerson, to Bob Phillips, who was most probably one of the best Bible teachers Donna and I had ever heard. Chuck had also helped to arrange bringing in Dr. Michael Brown, who was one of the most scholarly Jewish believers I knew of and who spoke regularly at Times Square. We loved his teachings. Michael Brown would regularly take on traditional rabbis in debate strongly exhorting Yeshua's position and with a great deal of love and respect, I might add, as they were not always pleasant toward him.

On one occasion, I visited Yale University for one of these debates, and Yeshua was greatly exhorted. After all, when you really start to look into the Hebrew Scriptures, it doesn't take too much time or effort to see the truth about Yeshua. Our problems as Jews is that we don't read our own book, otherwise we would have a lot more questions to ask.

In one of my first meetings with Arnie to discuss me joining the Jewish ministry team, I asked him how their intercessory[1] prayer meeting was, to which he replied, "We do not have one." My response to Arnie, "How can you have a Jewish ministry without effective fervent prayer?" He very quickly agreed that it was necessary for us to set this up. As a result, I agreed to join them as long as we could establish an intercessory meeting, and that is exactly what we did. The Times Square congregation had rented some office space across the street from the theatre that the ministry now owned, and every Wednesday morning, we would meet at 6 AM with all of the others in our group who were interested in joining us. Not long after, I began to teach on intercessory prayer, which also caused our weekly gatherings to grow.

Arnie and Joannie Klein had met the L-rd during the Jesus movement in the late 1960s and were now seasoned believers; they truly felt called to Jewish ministry. Arnie encouraged people to feel both free and comfortable in their spiritual gifts, and it was not long before the Holy Spirit started to show His presence in our meetings in some powerful ways. Shortly after, another friend of ours from One Accord joined us, Richard Davis, who was also a Jewish believer and had joined Times Square when it first started.

Those intercessory prayer meetings quickly became the spiritual highlight of the week, as G-d would show up in some unique manner and guide us into effective and fervent prayer for the ministry, or He would end up ministering to each of us as we needed it. However, the fullness of His presence was always with us, which is what made it so exciting. We could hardly wait until the next meeting to see what the Holy Spirit was going to do among us, and the fire began to catch around us. From this point the Jewish ministry truly began to flourish, which I began to manage with Richard Davis and another old friend from One Accord, John Vigario, who joined us a little later on. In addition, another new Jewish believer by the name of Doug Spitz joined our group and became a good friend. We had many outreaches in different parts of the city reaching out to Jewish people. In Times Square I also met and became really good friends with an actor by the name of Tom Wade, who has a great sense of humor and a very positive outlook on life, never giving up his goal and vision to succeed as an actor.

In one of the prayer meetings, Arnie and Joannie got their final call to make *Aliyah*[2] and return to Israel to start their ministry called Emmaus Way, which they are still managing today from Israel, almost twenty years later. When they left new York, Joannie changed her name to Yonit.

We began to organize outreaches through the Jewish Feasts, like we had done at One Accord, except this time we added other feasts, like Shavuot, which is the feast that celebrates the giving of the law at Mount Sinai. And not so quite incidentally, where the Church celebrates Pentecost, which is on the exact same day Yeshua sent the Holy Spirit, the very law of G-d to live in our hearts (see Jeremiah 31:33), the main key to the New Covenant.

The meetings were held at the chapel, across the street from the main theatre, where we also had a kitchen for food facilities. It looked like an office building, which actually helped us, as some Jewish people, simply could not walk into a church building. This time Donna was making and organizing food for more than two hundred at a time. Our meetings were always packed out, with a decent number of Jewish people coming to faith at every meeting we held—praise G-d. Chuck Cohen oversaw our work and we all reported into Don

Wilkerson, who became a great supporter of our efforts to outreach to the Jewish communities of New York City.

I also kept in touch with Richard Glickstein who was going through the adjustment of divorce and had moved his family back down to Nashville. I stopped over to see him when I visited one of my manufacturers in Lewisburg, Tennessee. My visit was very timely, especially as I shared with him all of the exciting things that were happening at Times Square with the Jewish ministry. It really raised his eyebrow, and he got enthused. He had just met Marcia, his wife to be, and they were dating, but he was definitely still struggling with everything that had gone on in his life. He lacked his usual zeal and zest for life that I had grown to love about him. Bob Jones, a well-known prophet in G-d's body, had prophesied to both of us that we would be involved with work in Russia, which, at the time we received the word in 1988, didn't make much sense to us. However, the Berlin Wall was now down and we were beginning to hear of a new movement of G-d's Spirit toward the Russian Jews, which we prayed about together and which really piqued Richard's interest.

The next year after he and Marcia married, he went back into full-time ministry and joined a group that was beginning to plant Messianic synagogues in the former Soviet Union. He and his family moved to Russia to help build this new Messianic work with another minister by the name of Mike Becker.

In the midst of all of these ministry activities, my family life was full, with Joshua keeping us on our toes and the business was growing nicely. In 1992 as I looked to expand Lord & Berry into the lip area and Donna's mother helped us to further fund the business, I developed a new product concept, known as lipstick in a pencil.

At that time, the early 1990s, matte lipstick[3] was all the craze. However matte lipstick was always dryer on the lips, because it usually had a much higher content of powders to kill the shine of the waxes. Looking to overcome this problem, I took note of a new product that one of my Italian suppliers had developed; they had presented to the major companies, but could not get any interest. Lipstick pencils were first marketed in the early 1980s; however, the formulas offered at that time had no distinct advantage over regular lipstick, and in fact they were most probably worse. So when the Italian pencil manufacturer, Fila, produced this new lipstick concept, it was quickly rejected. However, after clear inspection, I noticed a distinct advantage in the matte formulation, so I challenged the company to improve the formula and we started to develop this product concept together, while negotiating an exclusive on the product concept that no one else was interested in.

One year later, Lipstique, the ultimate lipstick, was born; and as soon as it hit the counters in the spring of 1993, it became a phenomenon, selling out everywhere within less than two weeks of being on the counters.

We quickly encountered a supply problem that we were never able to properly fix, and the demand kept growing before we could ever meet the supply. Cosmetic pencils take a lot longer to produce than other cosmetic products like lipstick, for example, and twelve to sixteen weeks lead times were pretty much the norm. I had never in my life seen a product sell like this so quickly, the consumer could not get enough of it. And all of a sudden, Lord & Berry mushroomed into the limelight.

We were still living on 24th Street at this time, still printing out all of the orders. And bringing them down to Rod, the garage attendant who was shipping the product from his home, which by now had almost turned itself into a warehouse, with several people working out of it. He was not complaining however, as he liked the extra money that he needed for his family. Rod was a great guy and a really hard worker, always dedicated and knew nothing less.

Joshua was now three years old and hitting the walls of our little apartment, which we also used as an office; we were beginning to bust out of our apartment. We were just beginning to make a decent living with our newfound success, but we were reinvesting everything into its growth, so we did not have any savings, but really needed to move.

One day I was visiting a buyer by the name of Ina Lenoff at the Century 21 department store in downtown Manhattan. We started talking about the best areas to live to raise a family and she had fallen in love with a number of the towns in upper Westchester County in New York State, which she really encouraged us to visit. That night when I got home, I mentioned it to Donna, and we decided to contact a broker there and visit the area. Since we had no savings and could not sell our apartment owing to the real estate bubble shortly after we purchased it in 1988, we did not think of purchasing a home at first and looked instead for rental properties in the area.

Ina was right, these little towns were just delightful, almost rural with more of a country style than a suburban feeling. However, the first time we looked, there was nothing really available, but spending time with the real estate agent, at least gave her an opportunity to know what we might like. Two weeks later, the real estate agent called Donna and told her about a brand-new townhouse development that was in the process of being built in one of these towns. Donna seemed really excited when I got home that night and already felt that it was G-d in her spirit; however, the homes were not for rent, but for sale.

That weekend we took a drive up to Armonk to see the house, and we both fell in love with it almost instantly, but we did not have enough money to make the 10 percent deposit. On that same day we met the builder, Mike Ferrari, who happened to be in the development at the same time, and we took a liking to each other. We also met another young couple Jeff and Jennifer Sencer, who were looking at the units at the same time, and have since become our dearest friends. Both Jeff and I were wearing the exact same pair of shoes, which was quite funny when you think about it and our two little boys Joshua and Ethan played together in the development.

The good feelings were all around us, but how was I going to find the money to pay for the deposit and who was going to give us a mortgage on top of the one we had for the apartment, when our income and credit history was so lacking. G-d's timing is key in our lives and when we live by faith and trust, doors can open and brick walls can fall that otherwise would not if we are too reliant on what we have and what we can control.

So I told Donna that we should at least pray about it, as she felt much stronger than I did that this was G-d's will for us and that we were supposed to buy the house. I just did not know how G-d was going to do it, and I had not yet heard from Him about it. So I started to fast and pray as we were really in need of more space at this point, and I knew we had to move. However, knowing G-d the way we did, I would never make this kind of decision without knowing His perfect will for us, which we can always expect as His children. We just have to learn how to listen, and by now I regularly waited on the L-rd for all major decisions and was not about to move an inch until I heard from Him, and Donna knew this about me, so she knew how to pray.

The very next week, Michael Brown was teaching a Bible study at Times Square and all of a sudden the Holy Spirit came upon Donna and I and told Donna that He was speaking to me about the house at the same time in the spirit. We were in worship and my eyes were closed basking in His most wonderful presence and His Spirit came upon me in a fuller way, and He started to show me several visions of the house with His name written in its foundation.

When G-d wants us to see something and people are praying, which my wife was, we can always expect heavenly results. And in this case we received very definite direction from above that indeed it was His will for us to buy the house, so somehow He would provide the money for us to make the deposit and take care of the rest.

When G-d speaks and you know it's Him, it will always happen, no matter what obstacles lay in front. The problem is usually with us, as we actually have such little faith when having to trust in matters that are out of our grip and control. In the New Covenant, it is no great surprise that G-d actually speaks to us. After all, if we have accepted it and consequently received the law of the Spirit of life into our hearts through Yeshua, which is what rebirths our spirits so that G-d may now dwell within each of us (see John 14:23). It is here that we get to know Him personally, as well as His voice and guidance. All of this was prophesied to us through Jeremiah with the promise of the New Covenant.

So learning to know and listen to His voice in the New Covenant is a process, which comes with trial and error in our new spiritual relationship and journey of faith. And G-d can speak to us in several different ways; through a still quiet voice that is different from your conscience, or even audibly. He also speaks through His Word, which will always confirm His direction to us. Sometimes His presence also comes upon us, as it says in His Word, when two or more are together with Him, there He is in the midst (see Matthew 18:20). He can also speak through others into our lives, but it is also wise to look for more than one confirmation, as we also have to learn to keep the enemy out, who will always try to deceive us. When he brings direction, it most often feels different even though it can seem close to the truth. Remember, the devil does not create, he can only coun-terfeit. So as John the apostle has informed us, we should always test the spirits and the words to know where they come from (see 1 John 4:1). We should always use caution when leaning on the Spirit, but we must also learn to trust Him as this is how He speaks to us, so we should not be afraid.

Yeshua was quite clear about this and told a Samaritan woman at the well on the way through Samaria (John 4) that the time was coming when we would worship in Spirit and truth. The truth is the Word of G-d and acts as a divine authority to guide us through life. However, please note that He put the Spirit first, as it is ultimately the Holy Spirit living in us who will shed light on the Word of G-d in each of our lives. And so balance is vital for a healthy spiritual relationship with G-d; and if one becomes out of balance, so will we.

The very next day, Donna's mother called us and offered to lend us the 10 percent deposit, and we could pay it back to her over a period of time—what a blessing! That week I also started looking for a broker to help us get a mortgage, which was not at all easy during those times. Not only were the banks very strict with credit in those days, but the country was just coming out of a recession and the real estate market was still in the toilet.

Getting a mortgage proved to be a serious battle for us and despite the broker's hard efforts and several months of work, the broker con-tacted us and advised us that the bank had turned us down and that there was nothing more he could do. It was now the beginning of the summer, and we were due to take possession of the property by the middle of September, so I started working with another broker, whose efforts also proved to be in vain. Now it was late August and we had run out of options, not knowing what to do, except to con-tinue to pray because of the clear words He had given us. By now we were very close to having to let go of the house, as we did not want to lose our deposit. It was almost the twelfth hour, which is so often the exact time G-d begins to move, because He is always wanting to build our faith and use our life experiences to sharpen us and make us stronger in Him.

Out of the blue, I received a phone call from the original broker and these were his exact words to me, which I will never forget, "Looks like this deal just got raised from the dead!" My spirit jumped immediately, I could hardly contain myself, "Hallelujah," I shouted out over the phone to the broker, who joined in the celebration. However, there was a catch. I now needed a 30 percent deposit to get the loan. "L-rd, where are we supposed to get the difference?" That summer I launched the new lipstick in a pencil concept and it was really selling way beyond my plans or expectations and I was able to take some of the funds from my business, but I was still short another 10 percent.

I had learned from my dad never to give up on anything so easily, and I was naturally persistent. In prayer one morning, the L-rd directed me to the builder. After all, the real estate market was still not strong and maybe he would be happy to keep me somehow? So I made an appointment with Mr. Ferrari in Armonk and went to see him.

In our meeting I explained my situation to him and that we wanted to buy the house, but that I was still 10 percent short on the deal, I was really honest with him. He replied quickly and decisively, "I will lend you the money on the balance." Again my spirit jumped and the final hurdle for us to buy and own this house had just melted away. I was very joyous in my spirit. He had been very kind and gracious, and we agreed on an interest rate, which was also very fair. I immediately called Donna to share the news.

The day we moved out of the city and into our new home, Joshua ran around every room, closet and bathroom, praising the L-rd for his wonderful new home, it was an amazing feeling of warmth and wholeness. I continued to run the business from home to keep expenses down, and we built an office in the attic of our new townhouse. We added two employees to help us manage the day-to-day business, as the lipstick pencil sales were continuing to explode.

Talk about a fire on a product! Wherever we placed Lipstique, it blew out. Now Asians, who had found out about our product on the West Coast, were going into our beauty supply accounts and buying out full racks at retail, then selling it for four times the price in Taiwan and Hong Kong. Women couldn't get enough of it; they loved the look of the matte lipstick and yet it was almost as creamy and moist as their regular lipsticks.

These were both exciting and challenging times, as the business was growing and expanding so quickly on so many fronts. I was now working over seventy hours a week trying to keep up with it all and traveling either in the U.S. or internationally every other week. It was like chasing a tiger by the tail, never really being able to catch and tame it. It wasn't long before we had to move the office out of the house; and Mike Ferrari, the man who had built our new home, built us warehouse space in one of his office buildings on New King Street in White Plains so we could consolidate our office and warehouse in the same location. I also loved the street address and thought it was a great tie-in to Lord & Berry.

In 1994, we sold over three million units and added twenty new employees, both in management and warehouse staff, and we started an expansion into a full cosmetic brand to further build the business. G-d's hand was truly upon this little brand, and we were beginning to get noticed everywhere!

ENDNOTES

1. Intercessory: To stand in the gap, between an issue or people and G-d.

2. Aliyah: The Law of return to Israel.

3. Matte lipstick: Lipstick that has no shine.

Chapter 16

BIRTH AND REBIRTH

Meanwhile, Donna and I were praying about having another child. One night as I was walking Boo-Boo, the L-rd told me that this was the night the child was to be conceived. I immediately rushed home all excited and shared the story with Donna and she was getting the same sense from the L-rd. Isn't it funny sometimes how G-d can intervene in our lives in our New Covenant relationship—and sure enough, that was the night that Donna got pregnant.

For some reason Donna thought we were having a girl at first, even though we had gotten a word from the L-rd a couple of years earlier that He was going to give Joshua a brother like King Saul's son Jonathan, was to King David, who loved him as his own. However, we had forgotten this and after visiting the doctor's office for a sonogram, we could not help notice the baby's privates on the screen! As soon as we left the office, the L-rd immediately reminded me of this word and I shared it with Donna. Right then and there, we decided to name him Jonathan, who was born on December 29, 1994. At eight pounds and fifteen ounces, Jonathan Dylan came bouncing into the world and was our biggest child.

Earlier that spring, Richard Glickstein had contacted me and invited me on an intercessory prayer trip to the former Soviet Union, which I immediately felt led to join. As a result, I connected it to one of my business trips visiting my Italian supplier in Italy, as I did not have much time to spare owing to the growth of my business. During this time our intercessory prayer group had intensified, the Klein's had already been sent off to Israel to start their ministry, and the Holy Spirit began to switch our focus to praying for the Russian Jews, even before I went on this trip. We also started to feel a connection with the land in Russia, regularly petitioning G-d if we were to take our Passover efforts there, which we were now successfully presenting at Times Square. By now the L-rd had also really bonded Richard Davis, John Vigario, and I in leadership, and He placed a unique unity and love between us, as if we were indeed a unit; it was great working with them.

Our prayer time with the others was definitely the spiritual highlight of the week, full of His power and His presence and guidance to pray for the Jewish people. We were now very curious as to what the L-rd wanted to say to us, and we had a strong sense that there was a connection here with this Russian trip. I couldn't wait to finish my business meetings in Italy, I was so excited and picked up a transfer flight through Frankfurt to Belarus. Richard had arranged for us to join the intercessory prayer team for a new Jewish ministry called Hear O Israel (headed by another Messianic Jew, Jonathan Bernis) for the first part of our trip.

As soon as the Berlin wall came down in 1989, G-d had given Jonathan Bernis a burden and idea to hold Jewish Musical Festivals in the former Soviet Union to help gather the Russian Jews. His first outreach was held in St. Petersburg and it just exploded, with thousands of Russian Jews coming to faith. This next outreach in Belarus was to be his second festival, a few months later. They were in need of prayer intercessors to help undergird the work, which is always a vital ingredient for any evangelistic effort, as prayer fuels the works of heaven on earth, something we Jews need to learn so much more about in the way in which we live our lives. This is not reading or citing repeated prayers, but rather speech and cries from deep within us, which make such a difference in the New Covenant, because G-d is always moved by the heart.

Arriving in Belarus was quite a culture shock. Not only was it very cold and grey, but it was almost third-world-like with many of the buildings seeming to date back to a time when money had run out; it was quite a peculiar sense and feeling. It almost felt as if time had stopped. In the taxi ride from the airport, I could smell the fumes coming up from the 20-year-old engine through the middle of the driver's gear box. However, despite the fumes, as I looked out the window, I started to weep. Deep down in my spirit I could feel this cry of my people coming from the land as I passed it by on the highway; and then I realized that I had many ancestors who had lived here, before coming to England where I had grown up. I joined the conference in its second day with my close friend Rex Duval, and between prayer sessions we rested and got reacquainted.

The Belarusians welcomed us with open arms; and frankly, after seventy years of communism, anything was a breath of fresh air. However, for a limited amount of time, Americans found great favor in the former Soviet Union, and so conducting outreaches was not as difficult as it may have appeared—plus the interpreters were happy to work for just a few dollars a day, and the American dollar went a mile everywhere. Having had the experience of the other outreach, Jonathan Bernis wanted to rent the largest concert hall in Belarus, seating over five thousand people, yet even this was not big enough! At show time, not only was the place completely packed out, there were thousands of people outside who could not get in.

Famous Russian and American singers—Victor Klimenco, Jonathan Settel and Marty Goetz, to name a few that I can remember

—were brought in to entertain the people with singing and dancing, and then toward the end of the evening, Jonathan came out and explained the reason for his coming to Belarus.

Jonathan Bernis had a very gentle spirit and was a humble man of G-d. He also looked like a Russian Jew, which I am sure helped the people to relate to him. G-d had definitely raised him up and prepared him for this remarkable time. When he walked out onto the stage, he very simply explained the message of Yeshua to them; and at the end of his speech, he invited people to come down to the altar if they wanted to ask Yeshua to come into their hearts in fulfillment of the New Covenant.

The response was unbelievable with thousands of Jewish people coming to faith. I had never witnessed anything like it in my life, nor had I seen so many Jewish people respond so effortlessly toward G-d. Back home in the States, most Jewish people were still so hard and resistant to Yeshua, but here there was no resistance at all, and I knew there and then that this was a sovereign work of G-d. While communism may have tried to steal faith from the people, it had wiped many Jewish souls clean of any animosity toward the name of Jesus, that back home and in the West was still so prominent in our minds and souls.

These people knew hardly anything about their Jewish heritage and were so thirsty for faith; we could feel it all around us. Many of us left the theatre to share and witness our faith to those outside who could not get in. David Levine, who was also one of the main organizers for the event, was preaching on a bullhorn and people were coming to faith all around us. There was definitely something quite supernatural happening, and I thought of the Scripture in Joel where it speaks of the last days and a unique outpouring of G-d's Spirit (see Joel 2:28-32). We were definitely caught up in a very special time and many of us had a sense and deep conviction that we were in the midst of the very fulfillment of Jeremiah's prophecy where G-d promised to bring the Israelites out of the land of the north.

> *"However, the days are coming," declares the L-RD, "when it will no longer be said, 'As surely as the L-RD lives, who brought the Israelites up out of Egypt,' but it will be said, 'As surely as the L-RD lives, who brought the Israelites up out of the land of the north and out of all the countries where he had banished them.' For I will restore them to the land I gave their ancestors"* (Jeremiah 16:14-15).

The ministry also began to help the Jews make Aliyah back to Israel, and during this time more than a million Jews left the former Soviet Union and returned to Israel or immigrated to the United States. When you see G-d's Word actually taking place right in front of your eyes, it does something unique to your faith. These words seemed almost unthinkable a few short years before, and all of a sudden, almost the entire Jewish population around us was being touched with the message of Yeshua and salvation and being stirred up to return to Israel.

There is one thing that we can definitely count on and that is G-d's Word is not only true but whatever is written in it, will come to pass. Now sometimes to us (humankind), His Word is subject to different interpretations, but not to G-d, who has the perfect understanding of His Word and all of the prophecies that are written. Although they may sometimes be a mystery to us, they are most certainly not to G-d. However, when you see Scripture being fulfilled right in front of your eyes, the mystery is no longer there, because life and history's timing has brought it to pass, and it is then clear and evident for all to see.

This is indeed what it will be like before the Messiah returns, when all of the prophecies laid out in Scripture will no longer be a mystery and Israel will then be fully redeemed, once again knowing G-d. However, this time it will be in a unique and personal way as a result of Yeshua and the New Covenant He has given to all of us. This was also certainly the case with the restoration of the land of Israel, which was also a complete miracle.

Who could have ever believed that the land of Israel would be restored, except that it was written and prophesied in G-d's Word and that G-d would make it happen. To think that most of the world would come into agreement with this, despite the world's great anti-Semitism toward the Jewish people, and look what we suffered to help bring it to pass. Almost the very same death that Yeshua suffered, our people were forced into concentration camps and gas chambers and became like animals to humanity and were scourged unto death. Yet from this horrific death and persecution and for a very brief period of time, the world took pity on us and their hearts were turned to us with compassion. Through it, in an instant the nation of Israel was reborn, which is a partial fulfillment of Ezekiel's prophecy (see Ezekiel 37), where the dry bones came to life.

In February 2010, even Israel's own Prime Minister Benjamin Netanyahu declared this prophecy to be fulfilled, when speaking at a memorial conference at Auschwitz in Poland.

"Then he said to me: Son of man, these bones are the whole house of Israel. They say [as they would in those camps], 'Our bones are dried up and our hope is gone, we are cut off.' Therefore prophecy to them: This is what the Sovereign L-rd says: O my people, I am going to open your graves and bring you up from them: I will bring you back to the land of Israel. Then you my people will know that I am the L-rd, when I open your graves and bring you up from them. I will put my Spirit in you and you will live and I will settle you in your own land. Then will you know that I the

L-rd have spoken, and I have done it, declares the L-rd" (Ezekiel 37:11-14).

While we may have rejected Him in His first coming, it definitely seems that as His first-born children, we have also suffered like Him. Although I cannot fully explain this, there has definitely been some correlation between the suffering of the Messiah's first coming and Israel's Diaspora experience. The Isaiah prophecy (see Isaiah 52:13–53:1-12) very uniquely describes Yeshua's first coming. How accurate a picture these words were of what Yeshua actually lived and suffered. All of Christianity sees the clarity of this prophetic Scripture in Yeshua's life and ministry, and I completely agree with this interpretation.

However, some Rabbinic Rabbis who at this point still do not believe in Yeshua, see Israel's suffering as its interpretation. And with all that our people have suffered, I can well understand how they feel and definitely understand their perspective. Through suffering and death, Yeshua brought redemption, spiritual life, and peace from within. Through suffering and death, the Jews redeemed the land and brought it back to life.

Now here in the land of the North, at the Hear O Israel Music Festivals, this was certainly the case too, with G-d now beginning to fulfill the second part of Ezekiel's prophecies (see Ezekiel 36-37), where the Spirit of G-d is breathed into the hearts of the Jewish people. We could hardly believe our eyes as we were witnessing this firsthand. However, this prophecy is yet to be fulfilled to the entire nation of Israel and the Jewish people around the world. For while Israel has been restored as a nation, it is now in the process of being rebirthed spiritually and Jewish believers today are still very much a minority. But make no mistake, the spiritual awakening has already begun and it will only increase as we draw closer to the L-rd's coming. We know now that this was just the beginning, and seeing Jewish people touched by the presence and power of G-d in so many numbers has changed my faith and perspective forever, as I know now for sure that the rest of Israel's enlightenment is just a question of G-d's plan and timing (see Romans 11).

When we believe in Yeshua and accept G-d's plan of salvation for our lives, His Holy Spirit, the *Ruach Kodesh,* comes to live within our hearts. He then begins a process known as sanctification and starts to clean us up from within. This is a most unique faith experience and spiritual journey that each of us embark on, as He establishes more of G-d within us (see John 14:15-23).

Remember, He made each of us so uniquely that none of us are the same. And so is it with our walks of faith. We begin a spiritual journey and adventure that is also unique in the way in which He will use our lives to transform and heal us. This is why our New Covenant relationship with G-d is so personal and intimate and why knowing Him from within is so crucial to the success of our individual walks. G-d has promised us a guide, and we must learn to understand how He will lead each of us in applying His character of love and faith to our lives.

Things that may have gripped and controlled us from our pasts, especially fears and depression, can now be removed and healed, for truly He is the great Healer. When we give over our hearts in trust to Him, He can begin to move mountains in our lives, which is the power of the New Covenant that has touched my life and can touch yours, even as you are reading this book.

While we were in Minsk, we paid a visit to one of the memorials sites; Zaslavskaya,[1] which was later rebuilt to remember and honor those who had died there. On March 2, 1942, five thousand Jews from the Minsk ghetto were rounded up by the occupying Nazi forces and shot—they fell into the pit they had been made to dig themselves. Not everyone died from the shots fired; a large percent-age of the Jews were buried alive; it was reported that screams could be heard from beneath the dirt of the pit even two days later. We wept and wept as we remembered this horrific act. Bruce Cohen, another Jewish believer, became our tour guide for the visit, and he led us in prayer.

Hear O Israel Ministries also held special banquets for all of the Holocaust survivors in each of the cities the ministry visited. I attended one of these lunches and witnessed for myself firsthand the power of the Holy Spirit falling upon these wonderful older Jewish people who had suffered so much. Yet what was different here, was instead of them blaming G-d, G-d's full presence was sovereignly touching them as many of them received Yeshua for the first time. The weeping and the cries were so great in the room that I could not escape it, and I wept with my people, as they received G-d's love into their hearts. They were also honored at the Festivals as they were brought up onto the stage.

The Messianic movement was growing, and many young Jew-ish and Gentile spiritual leaders were drawn to these outreaches to witness the move of the Holy Spirit among the Russian Jews. It had wonderful effects on many of us who attended. New ministries were birthed from it, as our faith was being taken to new levels as we began to see G-d working in a greater way among the Jews.

We need to understand that Messianic Jews are caught between two main groups. The Jews, who do not yet accept Yeshua as the Messiah and all of the issues that go along with that, and the Church, who, for the most part, does not really understand us and expects us to become Gentile like them. So we are often used to misunderstand-ing and discouragement, and as Jewish believers we have to learn to deal with that, as it goes with the territory. However, this new awakening was like a breath of fresh air to all of us and it greatly strengthened our movement.

For the past fifteen years the Messianic movement had been in its infancy and to a certain extent, as it was growing and expanding, it was also trying to find itself. As I stated earlier in the book, I was not that comfortable in a Messianic congregation when I first believed in 1985, owing to the religious experience. Plus it is the Spirit of G-d in the New Covenant who brings liberty into all things, even Jewish styles and frames of worship. I was personally so turned off by the dryness of religious liturgy from my own synagogue experience as I was growing up in England; I could not go back to it even in a New Covenant Messianic setting that many Messianic groups were practicing at that time.

However, in their defense, the Messianic movement was so infant and young, that in stepping out toward Yeshua, many also wanted to be sure that we would not leave our Jewish identity behind, which was essential to us as Jewish believers. Since those early days, I am pleased to say that the Messianic body is growing up and many Jewish leaders have been finding greater balance between their Jewish heritage and the New Covenant relationship with G-d in His Holy Spirit.

While we now are more comfortable in the fact that there is still a place for the Jews and for Israel in the New Covenant, and a rather significant one I might add, we are also becoming more keenly aware of the unity that our G-d desires to have with all of His children, both Jew and Gentile alike, and this is true for the Church as well. This unity, I believe, is very close to G-d's heart, that we would be one in Him and live as a family under His loving umbrella, with G-d's full blessing for both groups (Jew and Gentile believers) to live out their calling and identity in Messiah. For this is G-d's love that we would be one spiritual family with unique and distinctive calls, just like the many differences between the children in any family, or a husband and wife that Rabbi Paul refers to in his letter to the Galatians (see Galatians 3:28).

While there is a oneness in the Spirit, there are still differences in our callings as Jewish and Gentile believers. However, more change is needed in the Church in order for G-d to bring this about. As more and more of us Jews are coming to faith before the L-rd's return, perhaps G-d's Gentile spiritual family could consider being more like the Jewish apostles and fathers of our faith who heard the voice of the Spirit in opening up to the Gentile world and reacted accordingly. For Jewish believers are indeed called to live as Jews and the Church must learn to bless them in this so they can properly reach their own and more importantly fulfill G-d's covenants call to them, which is essential for Yeshua to return. Please keep in mind who is grafted into whom.

Today, many of the newer Messianic congregations that are getting established are more grounded in this position of faith, which is known as the "One New Man" and seeks to promote both unity and love between both Jewish and Gentile believers and to which I personally ascribe. While both Jews and Gentiles now have equality in the Spirit of G-d, this does not mean that G-d does not still have distinctive roles for each of us to play and especially for the people of Israel, who must be spiritually awakened before Messiah can return. For has not Yeshua told us that He will not return, *"until you say blessed is he who comes in the name of the L-rd,"* meaning the Jews (Luke 13:35).

This is why it is so important for us as Jewish believers to both maintain and continue our heritage by continuing to live as Jews, and this not only needs the Church's support, but its full blessing as well so that Israel can be reestablished into G-d's covenants, to show His glory to the nations (see Ezekiel 36) by honoring His Word and promises to them—because He cannot deny Himself.

I also believe that G-d is looking for His Church to get much more involved in this than they are presently. To help rebirth my people spiritually, through prayer, intercession, and lifestyle evangelism, to show the Jewish people, just how much they really do love them and want to be joined with them spiritually in these days.

As we move toward Messiah's return, this issue of Israel and its people and the reuniting of G-d's spiritual family will become the most significant issue for the Church and G-d help those who remain indifferent. To re-quote Rabbi Gamaliel paraphrased, *"For if this work is from G-d, you will not be able to stop it, you will only find yourselves fighting against G-d"* (see Acts 5:39).

These issues are the main topic of my second book, *The Father's Heart for Israel and the Church—Where Do We Go from Here?* And if you are interested in learning more about this subject, I would strongly encourage you to read it.

ENDNOTE

1. "Zaslavskaya," http://www.flickr.com/photos/11683866@N06/3451251818/; accessed April 23, 2012.

Chapter 17

THE PASSOVER CALL

This was only the first part of our trip to the former Soviet Union, and we were already filled and overflowing with His presence and power in our hearts. The second part was to be spent in Moscow, so we could intercede and pray in the heart of the country. There were approximately twenty of us in the group. Most of the airplanes into Belarus were modern jets; however, as soon as we boarded the plane to Moscow, it seemed like we went back in time by about fifty years. The airplane had a propeller engine, and it looked very much like one of those planes in an *Indiana Jones* movie—it was definitely very old.

I was seated by the window by one of the wings, and after we took off, I could not believe what I was seeing—a huge gash in one of the tires of the plane. I was quite an experienced traveler by now, not just with my family growing up but regularly traveling worldwide for my business—and I had already been in a couple of close situations. However, there were many in our group who had not flown very often, and I knew if I shared this information or brought it to the flight attendant's attention, most people on the plane would get very nervous. So I decided not say to anything; but from that moment forward until the time we landed, I prayed for a safe landing asking

G-d to send His angels to surround that tire, which I thought could not handle the landing.

Thank G-d for prayer, as it really does change things and circumstances. If we really knew how much our faith can really alter situations and circumstances, we would all spend much more time in prayer. Sure enough, as we landed, the tire splits even more and another large chunk of rubber fell away as the tire hit the runway. Now there was hardly anything left of the tire and yet what little was left of it still managed to hold together as we came to a full stop. I could not believe it and thanked G-d most profusely. I was most relieved and sincerely grateful that we had arrived safely; and I was very happy to exit that plane.

On the first day, we visited the Kremlin and Red Square and took in the historical sights and gathered together for prayer between sightseeing. On the second day, which I was very excited about, we had planned to visit the only two synagogues still standing in Moscow as in the days of communism, any construction of synagogues was strictly forbidden.

The first was the Choral Synagogue that was now mostly restored. It reminded me of some of the synagogues in Western Europe, except with a Russian influence in most of the décor. It was a beautiful building, but I did not sense any spiritual connection here. However, little did I know what was ahead of us as we traveled to the second location, which was about an hour's bus ride through the city.

We exited the busses and walked toward the synagogue area. When we got there, the entire area had been fenced and barricaded to the public. Much to all of our disappointment, the synagogue had been burned down in an anti-Semitic attack earlier that year in February, and it looked as if we were not going to be able to visit the site.

I have to say that I was quite disappointed, as the visits to the synagogues for me were probably the most significant on the entire prayer trip. Suddenly, and I don't know what compelled me, I thought to myself, *I have not come this far not to be able to visit and pray over this synagogue, especially since it had been destroyed through an anti-Semitic act.* Then I immediately climbed over the iron gates and looked around to see if there was any security on the premises—there was none. The coast was clear so I went back to where our group was waiting and found a way to open the gates, and we all went in. Almost the entire synagogue was burned down, with half the individual rooms remaining. All around us were burnt, charred remains of this house of G-d.

In our prayer group back home, we were seeking G-d's direction whether we should bring the Passover presentation to Russia and the former Soviet Union in light of the newly opened doors, and it was in this little burnt-down synagogue that the Spirit of G-d had decided to confirm this direction to us. As I walked in and out of each burned room, to the side of the main sanctuary there was a smaller room that may have been a library or a smaller teaching room. However, the room was filled with burnt, wet books and literature piled up upon one another, and it was now raining on top of everything else.

As I looked on top of the pile, I could not believe my eyes—right in the middle of it was a Passover Haggadah, in vibrant colors, and in English and Hebrew the cover read, *The Complete Story of The Exodus, The Passover Haggadah.* Right next to it was five hundred rubles. (See Picture at the back of the book).

This scene almost reminded me of one of those black and white television or print advertisements, where only the item being promoted was in color. Both the fire and the rain and the grayness of the current weather had severely dimmed everything around us and all of the burnt books and literature looked so dull and dead, almost as if they were black and white—yet this one Passover Haggadah seemed like it was neatly placed there up on top of the pile, it stood out conspicuously. As I reached down to touch it and placed my hands upon it, my spirit started to weep and the tears gushed down my face as the presence of the Spirit of G-d came all over my body and He started to speak to me.

In the New Covenant we have true intimacy with G-d, and while His Spirit now lives within us, the Holy Spirit can also visit us. Yeshua told us that the Holy Spirit is like a wind and He comes and goes as He pleases, so when people gather in His name, His presence will often come into the midst of those who are focused on Him. Indeed, there are also times when we as individuals can feel His presence and visitation, and this was definitely one of those clearer moments for me as I could feel His presence all over me. The moment I touched the Haggadah, He spoke to me in the Spirit and told me that I was to bring the Passover to Russia and that the money was a sign that He would provide it. I will not know until I am in heaven who placed the Haggadah and rubles there, but it would not at all surprise me if one of G-d's holy angels put it there, as it definitely looked like it was there for me, awaiting my arrival. This was no coincidence, I can assure you.

Unbeknowst to me at that time, some of the others in the group, Jim Goll and David Fitzpatrick, had cleared away some of the rubble in the main sanctuary and around the altar of the synagogue. We gathered there in prayer and intercession for the Jewish people. Jim Goll, who was one of the prophetic brothers in our prayer group and who is very gifted in this area of ministry, strategically positioned three of us Jewish believers right in front of the altar, and we began to pray. However, this was not a normal type of a prayer meeting and the best possible way for me to describe it, is that something strategic was going on in the heavenly realm as we prayed and interceded for the Jewish people. I could really feel the thunder of heaven working its way through us.

This was quite definitely one of the most powerful spiritual moments in my life and we all had a sense that not only were the Jewish people being released from these lands, but something new was being birthed that would later make more sense to me after we had launched the Passover Story in Russia and Belarus over the next three years. It was an amazing prayer journey with special thanks to Richard Glickstein who organized the trip and Jim Goll and David Fitzpatrick who helped G-d usher in this direction for me and the group back home in New York.

That year was full of new life and new beginnings. Donna was pregnant with Jonathan, and we started to adjust to more of a suburban lifestyle with Donna making lots of new friends in our neighborhood. The business continued its rapid expansion, and we began to respond to G-d's call for us to take the Jewish ministry to the former Soviet Union. During this same period, Times Square made some management changes and both Pastor Don Wilkerson and Pastor Bob Phillips also moved in new directions. Don Wilkerson headed up Teen Challenge International and began to further build the Teen Challenge network overseas.

In light of these changes, we started our own ministry for the new Russian outreach and asked Pastor Don and Chuck Cohen to stay over us, so we would have a spiritual covering and accountability, which is necessary for effective ministry. There should always be others we trust to oversee our efforts and who watch over us spiritually, as in our humanity, we can all make mistakes. Don and Chuck really supported our ministry in this area.

We prayed for a name for the new ministry and Jackie Vigario, John's wife, came up with the name "Abraham's Promise," which we all immediately loved. We moved the prayer meetings to Richard Davis's apartment on 93rd Street, where we started to meet at 6 AM every Wednesday morning. I had regular work in the city, so it was never much of a problem to arrange my schedule around this day and time. In our prayer meetings, we were now definitely very focused on our future outreach with the Passover Celebration. These prayer meetings were full of the presence of G-d guiding us into the work and ministry that lay ahead of us. And by now we had a number of people in our group who had also committed themselves to the new ministry—everyone was extremely dedicated, with a deep understanding of the call before us.

In the past we had always served food at all of our Passover outreaches; however, using the traditional Seder format in Russia would not work, as there were simply too many people to potentially reach out to. As we sought the L-rd and prayed, He started to open our minds up to a new format for the event. With the huge response I had seen at Hear O Israel's outreach, we knew that this door had been opened for a period of time, and despite our limited resources, we wanted to open it up as much as possible so the L-rd could fill the house, just as He was doing with Jonathan Bernis's outreach. We decided to adapt the Passover story into a stage presentation and celebration. Then one of us would bring the message and explanation of the Passover, using the Passover story itself to explain the Passover's fulfillment through Yeshua.

As Messianic Jews, we embrace both Testaments into one Bible. The Old Testament, made up of the Torah and the Tenach, otherwise known as the Hebrew Scriptures; and the New Testament, which was mainly written by the apostles of Yeshua, as I have already outlined. However, without the New Testament, we lose one of the major parts of G-d's story to humankind—the giving of His Son and the New Covenant that He was sure to give to Israel first, before it went out to the world, even though most of us did not receive it at that time.

When we put both of these books together, something very unique happens, as the New Covenant is so often a spiritual fulfillment of many of the Hebrew Scriptures. This was certainly very true of the Jewish Feasts, where Yeshua and G-d's final plan of salvation and redemption are clearly portrayed through each of them. The Passover actually foretells two other very exciting stories and acts as a prophetic shadow to foretell the gospel message of the Messiah Yeshua, as well as His return to the world to be a reigning King—once as a Lamb and the other as a Lion.

In this writing, I focus mostly on His first coming; however, there are some great teachings that also tie the Passover into His return through the book of Revelation. One book in particular is by Dan Juster, who has become one of the most formidable Messianic teachers of our time, *Passover, the Key to the Book of Revelation*. This is a great read and teaching on Messianic times, as well as many of his other books on Messianic Judaism.

The Passover is like a mirror image, a divine portrait from Israel's physical experience through the Passover, to a spiritual fulfillment that ultimately offers all humankind hope and deliverance. As a Jew and a believer and follower of Yeshua, this really excites me, as it not only confirms the message of salvation through Him, but also acts as a bridge and a confirmation from the Old Covenant to the new one. Let me explain:

Israel was in bondage to slavery and there was no way out for them. We in the world are in bondage to sin and there is no way out for us. Not only do our sins entangle and control our lives, but they also keep us separated from a Holy G-d who will ultimately bring sin into account, so like Israel, we are trapped. However, in G-d's love for Israel, He sent them a deliverer, the man Moses. And in G-d's love for all of us, He has now sent us the G-d man Yeshua, who has delivered us from the power of sin. Both obviously moved in divine power. As Moses extended his staff, he demonstrated the power of G-d that unleashed ten major plagues on the Egyptians, as well as parting the Red Sea. Yeshua extended His hand miraculously in healing and deliverance, as well as breaking through every physical dimension that G-d had established in nature and on the earth. He walked on water, He calmed storms, He multiplied five loaves and two fishes to feed five thousand people, and He raised the dead.

Moses delivered Israel physically; Yeshua delivers us spiritually with peace from the inside, which He accomplished first, being the Pascal Lamb who has taken away our sins. For it was the blood of the lamb on the doorposts of each house that protected Israel from the angel of death, and so it is His blood that must be taken and sprinkled on each of our hearts to protect us from the coming judgment against sin. For before Yeshua can return to the earth as the Lion, sin will be brought into account (see Revelation).

The Torah tells us clearly that the atonement is in the blood and that without blood, there can be no forgiveness (see Leviticus 17:11). As a result, G-d had to make a sacrfice for us, in order to redeem us, which He did through the sending of His Son.

In this way, when we put our hope and trust in Yeshua, we will be spared the judgment that will ultimately come onto the world for its sins. Lest we forget that the G-d of Israel is holy and nothing sinful may enter His presence. For it is written in the Torah that nothing unclean can come into G-d's presence and survive; but when we put our trust in Yeshua, G-d sees the redemption blood of His Son on the doorpost of each of our hearts and in this way we can come directly into His presence. The lamb also had to be perfect with none of its bones broken; so also was Yeshua perfect in all He did, including keeping the law perfectly, as well as being sinless, so He could pay the final sacrifice for all humanity's sin, which the law was to expose. At twilight He was taken out of the city and just like the lamb, He was given to humankind so that His blood would cover us all! (See Isaiah 53.)

All of this took place on the Passover itself—coincidence or divine plan? And was it a coincidence that on the last Passover He celebrated while still with us on the earth, He took the two main symbols at the Seder table and broke the bread and said this is My body given for you. Then He took the wine and said, this is the New Covenant in My blood, which is poured out for you (see Luke 22:19-21). During the same Passover week, He rode into Jerusalem on a donkey prophesied by Zechariah, and all Jerusalem greeted Him with cries and shouts of Hosanna. "...*Hosanna to the Son of David! Blessed is he who comes in the name of the L-rd!...*" (Matthew 21:1-10). "*Shout, Daughter Jerusalem! See, your king comes to you, righteous and victorious, lowly and riding on a donkey, on a colt, the foal of a donkey*" (Zechariah 9:9). And at the end of the week on the exact date of the Passover itself, He was taken and sacrificed for all of humankind's sin (see Isaiah 53:6).

Yeshua came not only to fulfill the law that was given to Israel, but His sacrifice should have brought us to the end of the sacrificial system, because He did away with the old system, ushering in a new one. However, since the majority of Jewish people living today have not yet accepted the New Covenant, we have been unable to taste the new wine and the new spiritual life that G-d has planned for us. This is one of the main reasons why in current Judaism today, there is so little spirituality and hardly any intimacy. So much so that especially as secular Jews, if we are honest with ourselves, we actually have very little connection with G-d, and if we want spirituality, we go looking for it in the wrong directions, in the New Age or even through Eastern experiences; because with current Judaism, there is nowhere near enough spirituality, and it is all rather dry.

In addition, all of the prophets foretold Yeshua's first coming; and, if we would only read our own Scriptures, we would actually be keeping our rabbis very busy trying to maintain one of the greatest deceptions that was ever perpetuated. It is time for us to begin to expose this so we can properly examine the facts and return to our G-d.

When Israel marched out of Egypt, the Bible tells us that a cloud led them by day and a pillar of fire by night. Neither the cloud nor the fire left them and both also protected them from the onslaught of the Egyptians. Both the cloud and pillar are representative of G-d's Holy Spirit. When we put our trust in Yeshua, He will send His Holy Spirit to live in our hearts, so that we will know G-d in an intimate way. He will lead and guide us as well as protect us, in accordance with the prophecies in our own Scriptures (see Ezekiel 36:24-28). There is nothing we can do to earn G-d's salvation in our own lives, no works or acts. Sin has trapped us, just like the bondages of our ancestors in Egypt who had no way out from the mud pits, except they cried unto their G-d. G-d sent them a deliverer, Moses, who foreshadowed Yeshua, whom G-d used to pay the price for humanity's sins once and for all. There is nothing we can do in our own strength to receive G-d's redemption, because G-d was pleased to do it for us, and it can only come by faith. Like the Israelites, all we have to do is be still and put our trust in Him and He will lead us across the sea and into a new life full of His Spirit and His presence. He has become the Pascal Lamb, and He can take away our sins forever.

Through Moses's faith, the Red Sea was parted and Israel walked through on dry ground. In a spiritual fulfillment, faith in the G-d of Israel through Yeshua will bring the power of G-d into your own life—and you will be changed forever! In reality, none of us would be here today if our ancestors hadn't walked through the Red Sea, and sometimes we really need to think about this. It is one of the main reasons why Moses directed us never to forget this story as he knew that the faith and belief of it had to be passed down so it would remain real to us.

However, because our faith and relationship in G-d is so distant today, with very little connection to any type of spirituality, we modern secular Jews, who make up the majority of our people, live way too much of our lives just within the physical boundaries that G-d has set up for the world, because true spirituality can only come by faith. This is how He has indeed set up the world, which takes us out of control a lot of the time, which is something we have become extremely uncomfortable about. As a result, most of us cannot even fathom these types of spiritual dynamics because we need to be awakened first to properly understand how G-d truly operates, which is in the spiritual realm.

Therefore, most of us will simply try to write off any of the incredible things that happened to our people in Egypt, or in the desert and the Promised Land as stories or fables, because there is no place in our rational minds for the spiritual world. For up to this point, if we are truly honest with ourselves, most of us still lack the real connection that we need to have with our own G-d to properly connect to the reality of His power to bring these and other biblical events to pass, not only then, but also today in our own lives.

When we escape to the movies to see films like *Star Wars* or *Lord of the Rings* or even with television shows like "Lost," we can so easily accept the spiritual dimensions that are offered. But when it comes to our modern world as well as our own lives, there is just no place for the spiritual realm for most of us. How foolish can we be to think that life exists solely within the physical realms of what we can see, feel, and touch, and yet this is exactly how most of us actually operate, giving no credence to the spiritual world that is in fact all around us. Could this be because we lack connection with our own G-d and instead look for all of our answers too much from man's own strength and ingenuity?

Please think about waking up to your own relationship with G-d who can heal the issues of your heart, as you open up in greater trust to Him. Indeed, as you put your faith and hope in Yeshua, He will and can deliver you from all of your inner struggles, your fears, and the depression that you may be dealing with. When you meet Him personally and come to know Him the way He always intended, your life will never be the same again.

When you think about it, how can there be so much symbolism with such a divine connection between these two events—Passover and salvation with Yeshua—if there was not a Creator and a Designer behind all of it? And when you honestly read these texts, sometimes it takes greater faith *not* to believe in them! I respectfully submit that this is definitely not a mistake or accident, but rather a divine lay-out for humankind's deliverance from sin and ultimate salvation, and that is why it is called a New Covenant.

This is the Passover story[1] that G-d wanted us to tell to the Russian Jews so they would not only understand and get reconnected to their Jewish heritage, but they would also know that there is a spiritual Deliverer who Moses would have believed in himself (see Deuteronomy 18:15-17).

ENDNOTE

1. For more info about *The Passover Story DVD*, please visit my Website: reconnectingministries.org.

Chapter 18

RUSSIAN JEWS COME TO THE L-RD

Everything seemed to be coming together nicely in our outreach efforts, but how were we going to pay for all of it? Outreaches cost money. We had lots of traveling and organizing expenses, we had to hire interpreters, rent out theatres, cover room and board and then we had to promote the event.

G-d was truly blessing Lord & Berry and the business kept booming and expanding. Perhaps it had G-d's fire on it because He knew we needed to find a way to finance Abraham's Promise, as we certainly had no time to work on raising money for these events. As a result, both Donna and I were happy to be able to make this investment in the kingdom of G-d, to cover all of the outreach's expenses. That year the movie *Schindler's List* was released. This film truly exposes the horrible anti-Semitism of the Nazis in the Second World War. Oskar Schindler's business ventures were blessed during this time as he saved as many Jewish workers as possible from the hands of the Nazis, and we definitely connected here to our work with the Russian Jews. However, thank G-d we were not having to help save them from such horrific acts, but were rather helping them to re-find G-d and get back to the land. In fact, helping finance the outreach never became a second thought for us. It says in the New Covenant that we should build our treasures up in heaven where rust and moth do not destroy (see Matthew 6:19).

Our funding, however, was not unlimited as we also had to keep refinancing the business to meet its next phase of growth. I have to say though that G-d would literally take our five loaves and two fishes and multiply them into the direction of this ministry. When Yeshua was with us on the earth, there were often large crowds drawn around Him far from places to buy food. On one such occasion, Yeshua took the only food that the disciples had to eat, which was five loaves of bread and two fishes, and He blessed it and multiplied it. Miraculously, all in the crowd had plenty of food to eat, until they were fully satisfied—more than five thousand people ate of this heavenly manna on that incredible day (see Luke 9:10-17). This is how it honestly felt with our ministry.

That first year, the outreach was in Belarus and there were ten of us[1] in the Abraham's Promise group. All volunteers paid their own traveling expenses, room and board, and we covered the rest. We hired fifteen interpreters who were all believers from local congregations in either Minsk or other areas in the former Soviet Union, and they traveled with us and became our helpers. Most of these young interpreters were already on fire for G-d themselves and they were extremely happy to be involved in this work and learn more about their Jewish roots.

Aside from meeting for weekly prayer, we set up training meetings for all in our group and many of us were busy building the props and Passover story backdrop for the outreach. That first year, Richard, John, and I also wrote *The Passover Story*, which is now available on YouTube in two parts. It is a wonderful narrative work of the story of Passover told in a slide and musical presentation, which dramatically explains the Passover. Our goal now was to present the Passover through a stage presentation of two hours in length with a narrative telling the Passover story with singing and dancing. We rented two theatres in Belarus that seated approximately twelve hundred to two thousand people in each performance, one in Minsk, which is the country's capitol, and the second in another major city. The events would take place during the Passover season, so as to attract the Belarusian Jews. Toward the end of the performance, we would explain the fulfillment of the Passover, presenting the message of Yeshua, with all of its spiritual significance, and then give people a chance to respond to the message.

There was one lady in our group, Julie Mulliken, who was particularly talented in dance. So we asked her to organize the dance for the show and she started to train some of the other ladies in our group; Julie did an amazing job. For singing, we contacted Victor Klimenco, a famous Russian Cossack singer, who loved the Jewish people and whose songs and melodies were absolutely perfect for the Passover presentation. Victor had already been working with the Hear O Israel ministries, and he was very happy to join our efforts—what an amazing voice and singer!

For administration, we contacted a point person already in the land, who could help us make certain arrangements. Through one of my meetings in Minsk the year before, I was introduced to a minister by the name of Marty Huff, who became a strategic member of our team. He helped us get the events organized and was blessed to help the Jewish people in any way he could. There was hardly anything that he would not do for us; and I am not sure in that first year if we could have done it without him. He helped with the theater intros; he helped us to set up and coordinate of all of the interpreters, as well as anything else we needed. There were lots of different details, as you can imagine, trying to pull off an event of this size in a foreign land in such a short period of time and with so little help. We were also introduced to another Messianic believer named Stewart Winograd, who had just come to Minsk to start a new congregation; he also helped us with the outreach.

Spirit-led prayers and intercession really paved the way for us and opened the doors. So much so that when we actually went over there, we could really feel and sense it. It was like we were a special military force created for a specific target, and that's exactly how it felt. G-d was opening the doors and we were walking through them wherever we went.

The month before the outreach, Richard went over to work with Marty Huff to finish the last minute details, and John and I stayed behind working our jobs as well as managing and coordinating the last minute efforts on our end. Then John led the group on the trip, as I had a cosmetic show in Bologna, Italy, that I had to attend before the outreach. Donna did not join us as Jonathan had just been born a few months earlier, and we did not want to take any chances, especially not knowing what was really ahead of us in this foreign country and culture. I really missed her.

Believe it or not, our advertising budget was only about two thousand dollars that first year. So we really tried our best to promote the event through word of mouth. Therefore, we could not believe the response from the local Jewish community in each of the two cities where we held the outreaches. It was just unbelievable; we rarely had an empty seat in the house. It took us a little while to get properly organized with the presentation, with a few mistakes here and there, however, over the eight days of outreach in two cities, we presented ten different performances! Including two matinees on certain key days of the week. The Passover celebration was a smash hit, and all the people loved Victor Klimenco's singing, who was our main draw, as well as all of the dancing in the performance.

During certain numbers, both Julie and Victor would invite people up on stage to dance with them and the Spirit of joy filled the house. The Jewish population was also hungry to know about their past, and the Passover story was the perfect venue to help teach them about their own heritage. To this day, I will never know how this was achieved except for the work of G-d, but our audiences were always in the ninetieth percentile when it came to Jewish people, which was nothing short of a complete miracle. In addition and most importantly for us, the altars were packed with hundreds of Jewish people coming to faith in Yeshua through each performance.

I think perhaps, one of the greatest spiritual highlights for me was leading a 93-year-old lady to Yeshua; tears were streaming down her cheeks as she was meeting the G-d of Abraham personally for the first time. However, not only were the theaters packed, but the presence and peace of G-d was so thick that it flooded the stage and the entire building. Our prayer teams were busy for hours praying and counseling the many new believers. No one could deny the presence of G-d in those meetings, and this became a very real encounter for many Belarusian and Russian Jews as we continued the outreaches the following two years in 1996 and 1997. In some meetings, the presence of G-d was so strong that almost entire audiences would stand and respond to receive Yeshua as the Jewish Messiah into their hearts. Some of this is recorded on the DVD we made so that others could witness this move of G-d.

Like Hear O Israel ministries, we honored the Holocaust survivors and held special lunches for them, which was most appropriate in light of our outreach. We also honored them by inviting them on to the stage at every performance we held, and many of them came to faith in Yeshua.

In 1996, we visited Moscow for the first time and again the power and presence of G-d was with us at every junction to help these people find faith in G-d; the high response rate to Yeshua continued at every meeting we held. In one of our meetings, when attempting to reach out to the children, a young Jewish girl came up to me at the end of the meeting and gave me a penciled portrait of me speaking with her understanding of the event drawn in the picture. This time Don Wilkerson also visited the outreach, as he happened to be in Moscow at the same time working for Teen Challenge; he was greatly encouraged to witness this work to the Jewish people, which blessed his soul. His mother had always encouraged him to love the Jewish people.

Our budgets had grown by now, and John Vigario was now working full time for the ministry, helping to organize the events as well as coordinate those traveling with the group on the U.S. side who needed to be trained and equipped for the outreach. We also took a professional videographer, Rowland Bestwina, who I had known from One Accord on the 1996 and '97 outreaches. Diane Pearson joined our prayer and intercessory team, and also attended the '97 outreach, which was now organized by Eleanor Uttenwoldt, who had joined our prayer efforts at Times Square. Eleanor was a mature believer and acted like a spiritual mother to Richard, John, and myself over the three year campaign. She was a great blessing to us and the group.

That last year we were also joined by a number of believers from the local congregation Donna and I were now attending in Armonk, called Hillside. These new team members were Al and Agnes Sanchirico and Kent and Josephine Johnson, who we were later to get involved with in prayer for the Jewish people in the Westchester area. Both Donna and Joshua were able to join us on the third outreach, and I was certainly pleased to have my wife with me on this journey, which turned out to be both our largest outreach, as well as our last. Joshua also sang the Manish Tanah at our Passover dinner celebration for our ministry team, the last night we were in Moscow.

In 1997, we had our largest budget yet and rented a twenty-five hundred seat theatre in one of the most heavily populated Jewish neighborhoods in Moscow. However, this outreach was probably our most challenging since the beginning. This year we brought close to twenty people with us from the U.S. and hired over twenty interpreters for the outreaches. There was no question by now that we were quite effectively reaching the Jewish population and they were being drawn to the Passover Story, as it really was a terrific presentation for all to enjoy.

Word must have gotten out to the ultra-Orthodox community, and they were not at all happy with our outreach. On the first night of the event, there was a bomb scare and naturally we were all quite shaken by the threat. However, we immediately called in the authorities and after seeking the L-rd in prayer and having had the building thoroughly searched, we felt strongly from G-d that this was meant more as a threat to scare us to prevent the work from going forward, rather than an actual attack.

In addition, the Russian authorities very professionally took care of this for us; and in faith we decided to move ahead with the performance. Thankfully nothing happened and both our instincts and guidance from the Holy Spirit had been correct; the night was another amazing success, praise G-d! Both Victor Klimenco and Julie Mulliken did the singing and dancing for all of our outreaches; in the third year, Julie still performed while she was pregnant with her third child. By now, other Messianic leaders and Spirit-filled congregations joined our efforts with their full cooperation as they personally witnessed G-d's hand upon this work in presenting the Passover Story. Jonathan Bernis from Hear O Israel also joined us and recited the Aaronic Benediction over the people.

One of Marty's assistants, a young man by the name of Mark Hamilton, an Australian believer operated all the sound and electrical equipment for us at each of the shows, and we could not have done this without him. Mark became one of the regulars on our team, where he later met his future wife, Lira. To this day they have remained in Belarus working among youth for Young Life ministries.

Over the three years of outreaches, we presented the Passover Story to more than thirty-five thousand people, with many thousands of Jewish and Gentile people coming to faith. We also released the Passover Story to the Russian Jews, to hold their own outreaches with the presentation, which has already gone into several other Russian cities, wherever the Jewish people are still living. Hopefully to this day, the Passover Story is still being told in many other parts of Russia.

The political climate was once again beginning to change and that wide open door that many of us had walked through in the 1990s with both great favor and blessing, was beginning to close. Both the political and religious bodies were now looking to clamp down on any other work that was not sanctioned by the major religious groups, and many ministries began to lose their licenses to share their faith unless they were part of these organizations.

What I witnessed in the former Soviet Union with G-d's work and timing in revealing Himself to the Russian Jews would change my faith forever. I knew now that it was only a question of time and circumstances for the Jews of Israel and the West to be awakened to faith in Yeshua as His Word indeed foretold. We had witnessed the very fulfillment of Jeremiah's prophecy in awakening the Jews from the Northern lands and it was evident for all to see (see Jeremiah 16:14-15).

The accuracy of this Scripture, like so many others, should cause us to think twice about G-d's own Word and how telling it really is. For everything about us has been predicted including how it all ends. If we would only take a look for ourselves, we would be truly surprised by what we will find in the Word of G-d and why a great deal of the Gentile world has put its trust into our Holy Scriptures.

Before I end this first part of my life story and my introduction to the New Covenant, I feel strongly to properly explain a lot of what I now believe in a way that can hopefully bring more clarity and understanding to you in thinking about embracing Yeshua through the New Covenant. Aside from explaining the beginning from the end to help you better understand G-d's perspective, I have also addressed some of the touchier subjects regarding more sensitive Jewish issues along with G-d's final plans to show Himself through our people before Messiah returns and how it will actually effect all of us.

I hope you find this next chapter very interesting.

ENDNOTE

1. The ten names are credited on the Passover DVD.

Chapter 19

WHAT DO I NOW BELIEVE?

Part 1: The Covenants

Having now grown in the knowledge of Scripture, it has become easier for me to begin to overview the entire word of G-d and to recognize the different systems and covenants G-d had used to show Himself to us. Not only to make Himself known, but also to show His love to all of us. These covenants are best described through another Messianic brother's work, *The Eight Covenants of the Bible* by Dr. Arnold G. Fruchtenbaum. Dr. Fruchtenbaum very aptly describes these different covenants that G-d has made with Israel, as well as its commonwealth (Gentile believers) and His work can be easily accessed on the Internet. While I do not personally agree with some of his understanding on the law, as we transitioned from the old to the new, which I have explained more fully in Part 2, this piece of work is an excellent take on G-d's covenants and promises to Jew and Gentile alike. I have briefly listed and summarized these covenants, as I believe this will help us with a Jewish background gain a better understanding of G-d's total plan in revealing Himself to humanity.

The first was the *Edenic Covenant* (see Genesis 1:28-30; 2:15-17), where man and woman were first created by G-d and who actually lived in a paradise before sin was introduced into the world. It is important to note here that the world was very different before Adam and Eve sinned. I often think about how this dispensation maybe somewhat similar to heaven itself.

The second was the *Adamic Covenant* (see Genesis 3:14-19), where Adam and Eve disobeyed G-d and a result, suffered the consequences of their sin. This separated us from any intimacy with a holy and righteous G-d, who Adam and Eve had lived with in the Garden and known personally. Through this experience, our spirits died and came under a curse of spiritual death, which all humankind has inherited; in the process, the devil stole dominion of the earth away from us. The rest of Scripture clearly notes the consequences of sin to humankind, but more importantly lays down the path for humanity to return to G-d to ultimately be redeemed, who loves us with an unconditional love, but will never compromise the holiness of His character.

The next was the *Noahic Covenant* (see Genesis 9:1-17), where G-d raised up Noah to restart the human race because it was totally given over to wickedness. However, in Noah and his family, we see G-d's continued commitment toward humankind to save us from out of the world. Here G-d gave us the sign of the rainbow, His promise never to flood the world again.

Then came the *Abrahamic Covenant* (see Genesis 12:1-3; 13:14-17; 15:1-21; 17:1-21; 22:15-18) where G-d called out Abraham by faith to establish all who would believe, in Israel, as well as in the world. G-d gave him the Covenant of Circumcision, and Abraham's faith was credited to him as righteousness. G-d also confirmed His covenants through Abraham's lineage—through Isaac and through Jacob, who struggled with G-d and was renamed, "Israel" (see Genesis 26:2-6; 28:12-15; 35:9-14).

The *Land Covenant* (see Genesis 12:7; 13:14-15; 17:8; 28:15; 35:12 and Deuteronomy 29:1-30; 30:20), which G-d promised to the physical seed of Abraham.

The *Mosaic Covenant* (see Exodus 20:1–Deuteronomy 28:68), where G-d gave the law to Israel and brought sin into account.

The *Davidic Covenant* (see 2 Samuel 7:11-16; 1 Chronicles 17:10-14; Isaiah 11;1-16), where G-d established an eternal throne through the seed of David, which Messiah Yeshua will ultimately sit upon when He returns to the earth to rule the world.

And finally the *New Covenant*, where G-d circumcises our hearts with the new law of His Holy Spirit through the death and resurrection of Yeshua; both the Son and the Immanuel of G-d (see Jeremiah 31:31-34; Isaiah 7:14; 9:6-7; 52:16-53;1-12).

However, without the New Covenant our people have been lost into either extreme legalism through orthodoxy, or conservative and reform groups, most of whom are quite secular in their thinking, but are void of any true intimacy with our Creator, because we have yet to personally come into it individually as a people. While belief maybe sincere, both of these groups have theological confusion and are not clear about G-d, the world and its purposes, or about life and death. Not to mention atheism which denies any existence of G-d at all. Just like the Scripture says, *"The stone the builders rejected has become the cornerstone"* (Psalm 118:22).

In each of these covenants and dispensations[1] (systems), G-d had significant purposes for all of us, not only to redirect us, but to show us the way for us to return to Him. Lest we forget that the G-d of Israel is a holy G-d, a consuming fire, and nothing sinful may enter His presence. Yet, He is also a loving G-d who has given us both free will and choice in the hope and desire that we will want to choose to return to Him. Indeed it was His love that drew me back to Himself, which I now regularly feel inside because of my acceptance of this Covenant.

I believe G-d's desire was to use the covenants to establish faith in each of us, but also for us to fully recognize the barriers within our own hearts that separated us from Him. I believe G-d used the law to bring this to light, as it exposed the natural condition of our hearts, which was sinful toward G-d. However, G-d's Covenants did not end with the law, and unfortunately as a result, as a people we got stuck.

While most of these covenants were given to Israel, who will always play a distinctive role in the earth for His kingdom purposes, the truth of His Word and His salvation plan was never just meant for us alone, but would always be made available to everyone else. He just chose Israel first, as it was not yet time to reveal Himself to the world, which He would do later through His Son.

This is also clearly seen in G-d's covenant to Abraham and Isaac, which happened well before the law was given, where G-d promises that through their offspring and faith in G-d that all of the people of the nations of the earth would be blessed (see Genesis 26:4-5). For it is through Abraham and Isaac's seed, that all of the believing people of the nations now put their hope and trust, and through Isaac that the other covenants would come, which would ultimately bring Messiah.

We also need to understand that the Mosaic Covenant, was not the only covenant or dispensation[1] that G-d made with Israel. Yet, when you look at Orthodox Judaism today, it's about all you see. So many rules and laws to follow, but where is the intimacy and relationship that Abraham seemed to have with our G-d? Has it not been clouded by such legalism, that it is in fact extremely difficult to see the forest through the trees? As a result, modern Jews, who for the most part have rejected that legalism, are left with their traditions and very little knowledge of their own G-d. I can say this because as a secular Jew, this was my experience too, until I accepted the New Covenant, which immediately gave me intimacy with the G-d of Israel and reconnected me to the other covenants.

In fact, Scripture actually teaches us that Isaac was the child of promise (see Galatians 3:15-18; 4:23,28). Isaac was a special child and was abnormally born, for his mother was way past her years in childbearing. Yet as the story goes, G-d comes to visit Abraham and foretells of this happening, despite Sarah's own disbelief.

Isaac's life was used by G-d as a foreshadow of Yeshua's own sacrifice, as so many other Bible stories, also reflect other prophetic portraits of G-d Son's, who in reality is all over the Hebrew Scriptures, if we would just take a look and see for ourselves. For when G-d asked Abraham to offer Isaac, He never meant him to fulfill it, but rather was testing Abraham's obedience and faith. Yet a far greater picture came out of this amazing story than most of us in Israel have yet to see clearly. G-d used the story of Isaac to be a reflection of His one and only Son, who was also divinely born through the virgin birth.

For while G-d would not permit Abraham to go through with the sacrifice of Isaac and provided a way out, G-d was to later provide His own Son's life to be a sacrifice for all humanity, so that all of us could find redemption. That's why Yeshua is sometimes called the Isaac of G-d, because G-d willingly gave up His Son, who willingly laid down His life to be a ransom and paid the price for our sins. For in reality, love could never be truer than this, when we understand the truth of G-d's sacrifice because of His great love for each of us.

However, by the time Yeshua actually came, most of Israel had lost its real connection to the heart of the law, which was love, compassion, and mercy. Instead, they adopted their own ways of righteousness and were already extremely legalistic, which is also very apparent through the New Testament accounts of the Pharisees' behavior and responses to Yeshua Himself. As a result, our religious leaders rejected Yeshua, as both pride and control managed most of their hearts and blinded them to the truth and purpose of His mission.

There were a few in the Sanhedrin[2] who knew He was the Messiah and their hearts burned as they saw the other religious leaders come against Him. In fact, our own law had made us so separate, that we would actually have nothing to do with heathens (people who did not believe in the G-d of Israel), as we not only considered them unclean, but also beneath us. A spiritual pride had taken over our leaders, and it blinded them to the truth.

Yeshua told us a powerful story about compassion and mercy through a person who was attacked along the road from Jerusalem to Jericho that exposed this attitude. The man was robbed and beaten half to death. This story is known as "The Good Samaritan" and it really exposed the hearts of the Pharisees (who were the main religious group) toward strangers at this time in history, which Yeshua obviously did not agree with. Here both the priest and the Levite passed the injured person by, completely ignoring him. However, the Samaritan person, whom the Pharisees considered unclean, not only had pity on the injured person, but bandaged his wounds and got him safely to an inn, covering all of the costs to help him get better (see Matthew 10:25-37). Which of the three men did G-d's will, Yeshua asked.

Yeshua respected the authority of the religious leaders; however, He also exposed their hypocrisy. He told the people that we should obey them and do everything they tell us to do, "…*But do not do what they do, for they do not practice what they preach*" (Matthew 23:3). They were clean on the outside, but inside their hearts were in the wrong place, and Yeshua saw through them.

Yeshua also broke the tradition of not talking to heathens or even Samaritans, who were half Jews, and paved the way and transition for His Word to go out to the world, outside of Jewish circles, which the law somewhat isolated them from.

On a journey back to Galilee through the region of Samaria, Yeshua met a woman at Jacob's well, where He stopped to get some water. Here He ministered to her powerfully, telling her things about her life that only a prophet could have known, and she instantly believed in Him. He also shared with her perhaps the greatest truth of the New Covenant, that we would worship G-d in Spirit and truth, which best describes our position of faith in the new order. She then went back to tell others in her town who also believed in Him, that He was the Savior of the world, and many accepted Him and believed in His words (see John 4:1-42).

Belief in the New Covenant was also founded by Jews and none of them actually converted, they just crossed over into the next phase of G-d's plan, which was to bring the New Covenant to the whole world, which was just as Jewish as all of the other covenants G-d had made with Israel.

Yeshua's sacrifice and resurrection changed their lives, just like it was changing mine and this is why I was continuing to feel so Jewish in my heart, as Yeshua actually connected me to the G-d of my fathers, and I finally knew Him for myself, because He was now living in my heart. For Messiah was at the end of the Mosaic Law (see Romans 10:4) and ushered us into the New Covenant by laying down His life as a ransom for the sins of all humanity, something that most of our people just could not understand.

Put in another way, He became both our Yom Kippur and the Pascal Lamb, and His shed blood can now be placed upon the doorposts of our hearts that both protects and covers us from the judgment that is soon to come upon the world for its sins.

Our own Jewish feasts are so full of prophetic portraits and insights that points to this significance of Yeshua's ministry. He is also our Hanukkah, the great light that would shine in all of our hearts, and the New Covenant truly brings all of this into account. How much more Jewish could this be? Just read John chapters 9-11, where Yeshua is in the Temple in and around the Hanukkah feast and explains His mission to the Pharisees, how He is in fact the light of the world and the Jewish Messiah—but they would not accept Him. Despite His giving sight to a blind man and several days later raising His friend Lazarus from the dead. Not only did He want to show them that they were really the ones who could not see *"blind guides,"* but in the Lazarus miracle He proclaimed His resurrection and told the religious leaders that the power of G-d working through Him was all the evidence they needed to open their hearts toward Him—but they would not. The very last feast of Israel was to shine a prophetic light of both power and deliverance that would foreshadow the nativity, for He was to be the light of the world to shine from within each of us.

When He finally gave up His life upon that tree, it is written that the curtain in the Temple that separated the Holy of Holies and the Holy Place was torn in two from top to bottom (see Matthew 27:51). Before this, only the high priest was allowed into the Holy of Holies and only once a year on Yom Kippur. It was an incredibly Holy Place, as the presence of G-d rested upon the Ark of the Covenant and the Ten Commandments (which were inside the Ark), as it was not yet time for these doorways to be opened to humankind. In order to enter the Holy of Holies, the high priest had to take two blood sacrifices, one for Israel's sin and one for his own (see Leviticus 16). However, with Yeshua's sacrifice, G-d not only tore the curtain between the two places, but He made a way for us all to enter into the holy presence of G-d, to return to G-d, where we can all know Him for ourselves (see Jeremiah 31:31-34).

Yeshua Himself became our Yom Kippur. In the New Covenant, He sent the *Ruach Ha Kodesh,* the Holy Spirit, who already encompassed the law of G-d and circumcised our hearts so that we could know G-d intimately. His sacrifice freed us from the old system to introduce the new one. This was another spiritual fulfillment from the Hebrew Scriptures, where G-d gave Israel the physical circumcision, which prophetically pointed to the spiritual circumcision of the heart that G-d would bring to us all through Yeshua. If we choose to accept it, we ultimately will have the power to overcome from within and finally walk in obedience to G-d.

With Yeshua's coming, Judaism would be changed forever and we would no longer need or require a sacrificial system, as Yeshua's sacrifice was once and for all (Hebrews). G-d was moving on from the Mosaic Law, as He had done with a number of the other dispensations that He had made with man; and as I was discovering, this New Covenant was definitely superior to the old one (Hebrews). For the G-d of Israel was now living within me through His Holy Spirit, and I now had His power to overcome my weaknesses, which we did not have when we were called to keep the law, which is why we failed G-d in this place.

Just as Moses foretold (see Deuteronomy 28), G-d would now circumcise our hearts, for in the Old Covenant (Mosaic), the Holy Spirit only came upon humankind. In the New Covenant, Yeshua bought the right with His life blood not only to redeem us, but also to live within each of us, which is what happens when we open our hearts in trust to G-d.

Three days after Yeshua's sacrifice, after the curtain to the Holy of Holies was ripped in two, after He had taken on all of our sins, He arose from the dead to defeat the curse of sin and death that was upon us from Adam and bring us into the New Covenant. In this way, He was able to bring salvation to all humankind by establishing the New Covenant in His Son, as sin had to be atoned for in each one of us (see Leviticus 17:11), which the law actually required and brought to light. It was on the Passover, that He took two of its main elements, the unleavened bread and the cup of redemption and used them as symbols of the new life He was to bring to the world through His sacrifice and redemption.

Was it just coincidence that on the very Passover itself, His very own body was taken and offered as a lamb sacrifice for all humanity? I mean the timing of all these events is just unbelievable, for who could have arranged this except for G-d Himself? He took the bread, gave thanks and broke it and distributed it to His disciples. Then He said, *"This is my body given for you; do this in remembrance of me."* Then He took the cup of redemption to pass and drink, which was the fourth cup, saying, *"This cup is the new covenant in my blood, which is poured out for you"* (Luke 22:17-20), because through His sacrifice, He redeemed us (see Isaiah 53:5-6).

For G-d so loved the world that he gave his one and only Son, that whoever believes in him shall not perish but have eternal life. For G-d did not send his Son into the world to condemn the world, but to save the world through him (John 3:16-17).

John the apostle, the youngest of Yeshua's disciples and who also penned the great book of Revelation, wrote this about Yeshua:

In the beginning was the Word, and the Word was with G-d, and the Word was G-d. He was with G-d in the beginning Through him all things were made; without him nothing was made that has been made. In him was life, and that life was the light of all mankind. The light shines in the darkness and the darkness has not overcome it (John 1:1-5).

The truth of the covenants is that sin caused us to die spiritually, but as we journey through them in history and through His holy Word, we see G-d's love stretched out to each of us offering us both redemption and forgiveness so that we can all find and have fellowship and intimacy with a holy and righteous G-d. For when we accept G-d's Kippur (atonement) for us, His blood covers each of our hearts from sin's wrath and judgment, and His Spirit awakens us from the spiritual death that has come upon us all—and our spirits are actually rebirthed. This is why Yeshua told Nicodemus, who was one of the rabbi's in the Sanhedrin who believed in Him, that our spirits must be reborn, because sin and its curse had caused our spirits to be dead and separate from G-d (see John 3:1-21). G-d knew we had to be redeemed in order to return to an intimate and personal relationship with Him.

However, as we journey through the covenants from the beginning to the end, we see G-d's plan to win us back to Himself. There is nothing we can do in ourselves to earn G-d's righteousness, because each of us is sinful. However, Yeshua willingly laid down His life to be a Kippur for us all, and when G-d now looks down on me, He no longer sees my sin, but His own Son's blood that now covers the doorpost of my heart so that I can enter into the Holy of Holies and have intimate fellowship with the G-d of heaven and earth. Wow!

It is just amazing how G-d actually laid all of this out for us, but impossible for us to see when sin still blinds our hearts. *"For the message of the cross is foolishness to those who are perishing, but to those who are being saved, it is the power of G-d"* (1 Corinthians 1:18). The acknowledgment of our own sin before a holy G-d is truly the golden key to open this door in our lives. However, I had to choose Him and accept His Kippur for me before He would fully make Himself known to me; the G-d of Israel is sovereign, and thank G-d He is! For look what was now happening to me, once I made this decision. Without a doubt, it was the most important choice I will ever make in my entire life, and I will always be eternally grateful for it. Could our own hearts as Jews, actually be veiled to this truth?

Yeshua gave Himself up willingly, and He was the only One who ever kept the law perfectly. He was not born of sin, but born from above to become the perfect Lamb without blemish to take on the sins of the world, for it pleased the Father to offer Him up for us and that, my friend, is what love is really all about. Yeshua knew His greatest mission was to become a sacrifice, and despite the fact that most of us Jews do still not believe in Him, isn't it amazing how this one life has affected the whole world. Why can't we see this? As Yeshua told Pilate, the Roman governor of Judea, *You would have no power over me if it were not given to you from above. Therefore the one who handed me over to you is guilty of a greater sin*" (John 19:11); and look what happened to Judas (see Matthew 27:1-10).

At the right time, Yeshua told His disciples of the suffering that was ahead of Him; however, they just did not understand G-d's purposes for Him at this time (see John 13). Even when upon the tree amidst all of His sufferings, He calls out to forgive those who had placed Him there. Can you imagine how the religious leaders felt in their hearts as they looked upon Him? The very conviction they must have felt, as they heard Him forgiving them in the midst of His pain and torment, O my G-d! However, as Isaiah had foretold us, their hearts were hardened, so just like Pharaoh they could not see the truth.

Yeshua actually wept over Jerusalem:

Jerusalem, Jerusalem, you who kill the prophets and stone those sent to you, how often have I longed to gather your children together, as a hen gathers her chicks under her wings, but you were not willing (Matthew 23:37).

Fifty days after the Passover on the holiday of Shavuot when Israel celebrates the giving of the Mosaic Law, the New Covenant Law was released into the hearts of humankind—another coincidence, or by design? The Holy Spirit's power fell upon Yeshua's apostles and all of those witnessing the event. Their hearts were circumcised and the New Covenant began to spread throughout the world like a wild fire in a dry forest, to the Jew first and then to the Gentile, just as G-d had planned it.

Read it for yourselves in the book of Acts where it is written how Yeshua took a handful of Jewish lives and with the power of G-d now living inside of them turned the world upside down, or should I say, right side up! However, our religious leaders would not even listen, but instead deceived our people because of their pride and their blindness. Could they have actually liked their own religion better than serving and yielding their hearts to the One who gave it to them in the first place? And does not absolute power corrupt, for this is what our religious leaders had over us; they spoke, and we followed.

Read what Yeshua told them; for, if they had both listened to Him and received Him, things would have been very different!

And the Father who sent me has himself testified concerning me. You have never heard his voice nor seen his form, nor does his word dwell in you, for you do not believe the one he sent. You study the scriptures diligently because you think that in them you have eternal life. These are the very Scriptures that testify about me, yet you refuse to come to me to have life. ...But do not think I will accuse you before the Father. Your accuser will be Moses on whom your hopes are set. If you believed Moses, you would believe me, for he wrote about me. But since you do not believe what he wrote, how are you going to believe what I say? (John 5:37-40,45-47; see Deuteronomy 18:14-19).

As a result of understanding this Scripture passage, for a very brief period of time, I actually became angry toward our religious leaders, because they had led us astray, as I felt that they had hidden this truth from our people. However, it was not long before G-d used this in my life to release His forgiveness and love in me, which was what the New Covenant is all about—to help get my attention back on Israel, to begin to refocus on my calling back to my people who indeed I felt connected to and who I truly loved. In addition, I knew now that my people had been blinded spiritually (see Isaiah 6), and except for the grace of G-d in my life, I wouldn't be able to see either. However, that grace is there for all of us, from the least to the greatest among us, and G-d's heart greatly desires all of us to return to Him.

In light of our leaders' rejection of Messiah's first coming, Judaism was to be changed forever. Yeshua foretold of the Temple's destruction, that not one stone would lay on another (see Luke 21:5-6), and in the words of our prophet Isaiah:

> *...for both Israel and Judah, he will be a stone that causes people to stumble and a rock that makes them fall. And for the people of Jerusalem he will be a trap and a snare. Many of them will stumble; they will fall and be broken, they will be snared and captured* (8:14-15).

We were dispersed from our land because our hearts were distant from Him and because of our own disobedience to the calling of G-d upon us; we did not keep His law, which was much more about mercy and compassion than it was about sacrifice. Instead, our leaders looked to establish their own righteousness, which was not acceptable to G-d. So much so, that we were actually blinded to G-d's visitation to us through Yeshua and ended up rejecting Him, despite His many appeals. We rejected the only One who could have given us and still can give us the final redemption we truly need, because no man can properly keep the entire law anyway, except the One who fulfilled it.

And the Bible tells us that He kept it perfectly, so He could become the sacrifice for us all.

All of this actually happened to us, just like Moses had fore-warned (see Deuteronomy 28). However, G-d did not condemn us for His death. On the contrary, He gave up His life for us so we could live forever. However, because our leaders would not listen and submit to G-d's authority, we would no longer be allowed to live in the land and would have to experience the pain and suffering of the Diaspora.

This is an extremely difficult pill for us to have to swallow, but we must be willing to face the truth if we are going to embrace the change we so desperately need in our hearts. For we only have to look at the history of our people to see how it has actually played itself out. How the words of Torah about our dispersion confirm this and the journey and suffering we would experience are also extremely accurate, just as our re-gathering is also beginning to play itself out.

Part 2: The Purpose of the Mosaic Law

To start, we need to try and understand G-d's main purposes in giving us the Mosaic law in the first place. The Mosaic covenant was not the only covenant G-d would actually make with us, which is why we need to gain an understanding of all of the covenants so we can better understand how G-d has moved through them, which is crucial to our spiritual awakening. The Mosaic law gave us rules to live by, including universal moral standards that would help to protect and prosper us; and for its time, there was nothing like it on the face of the earth. Imagine, people being ruled by law? However, it also set us apart as a people, distinctly portraying the mark of G-d upon us as His very own, which was also part of His plan. Through circumcision and in all of the ways we lived and interacted with each other, the clothes we would wear and the food we consumed and how it was to be eaten, and in every aspect of our lives, the law placed a mark upon us so that we were to be a distinctive people among the earth, for G-d truly set us apart as His very own.

He also made unconditional covenants with us through Abraham and King David (see 2 Samuel 7:11-16 and 1 Chronicles 17:10) and He promised to bless us and give us the land of milk and honey, the land of Israel. One thing is for sure, G-d's Word is true, and whatever is written will come to pass, that I was now truly learning to bank on, and it was changing my life.

He has promised us an eternal throne given through King David that would not only seat David's son, but one day would seat the very Messiah Himself, where we would rule and reign with Him in righteousness. For while we have truly suffered as a people, there are still to come many great blessings upon the people of Israel along with the rest of our spiritual family, as we once again get reconnected with our G-d and embrace His New Covenant. However, as we will see, in giving the Mosaic Law to His first-born children, we then had the responsibility to keep it.

G-d also gave us a great period of blessing and covering under the law from the times of Joshua to the times of Solomon. However, Scripture also shows our constant disobedience, for we did not want to live up to our call and instead longed to be like the people of the world around us. However, the main purpose of the law was not just given to us to adapt certain codes to live by, but rather to expose the inner character of our hearts. For G-d established the law as a bridge to win us back to righteousness.

When we read the account of the Garden of Eden, we can clearly see that because both Adam and Eve disobeyed G-d, sin immediately entered them and they died spiritually. They had become like G-d, knowing both good and evil. As humans, we did not have the power in ourselves, like G-d, to constantly choose good; and as a result, sin took root in us and we died. Therefore, we had to be cast out of G-d's presence because nothing sinful can come into G-d's presence, who is holy and without sin.

In wanting to redeem us, G-d had to first establish a covenant that would show man his own shortcomings and give him constant reminders of his own character, which is why He also gave us a temporary sacrificial system, so we could find forgiveness for our actions while we were in it. After all, who of us could truly keep the Ten Commandments perfectly, every day of our lives? We cannot, because indeed we are human and the law actually mirrors our hearts and reflects our own shortcomings; but the system G-d established also allowed us to receive His mercy and His forgiveness while we were in it.

Indeed, the sacrificial system showed us that there must be a blood sacrifice for forgiveness and redemption from sin, for the atonement was in the blood. From Abel's sacrifice to the Pascal Lamb, G-d showed us the significance of the blood, as ultimately G-d would send His own Son, whose blood was shed once and for all to end this system and bring us into the New Covenant, so we could all return to Him, knowing Him personally for ourselves.

As modern Jews, we have long forgotten the sacrificial system, however without blood sacrifice there is no forgiveness for sin, as the Torah clearly points out to us (see Leviticus 17:11). G-d actually did away with the sacrificial system, as it was only meant to be temporary until all things were fulfilled through Messiah (see Jeremiah 31:32). Sin had to be exposed in us first, which the law achieved (see Exodus 19), so G-d could provide us a final act of redemption, which He did through His Son.

Are you beginning to get it now? Does this make more sense of G-d's purposes through the Mosaic law? And are you beginning to see the significance in having to receive Yeshua, who is the New Covenant? Without Him, we are still dead spiritually in our sins. For G-d did not send His Son to condemn the world, but rather to save us from ourselves! (See John 3:16-17.)

This is why the Mosaic law was actually a conditional covenant. The covenants with Abraham and David were unconditional, which means that the ability to bring them to pass belongs solely to G-d. However, both the Edenic and Mosaic covenants were conditional, which means we needed to operate in obedience to them to be able to reap the blessings that G-d actually gave through them.

I have to be honest here with myself, as knowing my inner self now the way that I do, I am extremely grateful that I was born at such a time that I could come into the New Covenant, rather than the Old one under the law. I now have the power of the Holy Spirit who lives within my heart to help me be obedient to G-d's edicts, because without it, who of us can really keep the law? Just look at the extremes that our Orthodox brethren go through in their attempts to try to keep the law; yet in many places, their hearts are just as sinful as the rest of us.

When you accept Yeshua into your heart, you truly begin to become aware of the reality of your heart condition, which is sinful, and a battle begins between your own nature and the nature of G-d as He circumcises your heart with His New Covenant law, where His Spirit is placed within you (see Deuteronomy 30:6). As a result, I could honestly see the reality of both the good and evil in my own heart, and I was now learning the truth about myself. I was also beginning to understand the concept of sin better within my own heart. Sin is not just the outward actions that we obviously think of when we think of it, such as murder or adultery or even stealing, which is why so many people do not think of themselves as sinful, because they think they are basically good, because they abstain from some of the major concepts of sin.

However, the Bible clearly teaches us that not one of us is righteous and all have gone astray falling short of a holy and righteous G-d (see Isaiah 53:6). This is why G-d needed to introduce the law before He could bring about our final redemption, and this is how indeed we can actually see the covenants in action within each of us. We are all in need of a Savoir, and without His shed blood, we remain under the curse of sin and death that separated us from Him in the first place. That's why we needed to be saved! Saved from a spiritual death that will ultimately come upon the whole world, except for those who have His blood on the doorposts of their hearts and have already been redeemed and brought back to life—those whose names are written in the Lamb's book of life (see Revelation 21:27).

We have all ultimately inherited a sinful nature from Adam that causes us to be separate from G-d. That is why Yeshua had to become our atonement, so we could return to the Father. As it says, He was the firstborn from the dead to defeat sins curse (see 1 Corinthians 15:20), so that we too may follow Him and become alive spiritually. However, despite the truth about our sinful natures and heart conditions, because we now can operate in the New Covenant, we become much more conscious of our inner selves, especially when we know the truth about ourselves, and as a result our knowledge of sin greatly changes. Not only so, but when we accept Yeshua's Kippur, we have the power to be free of sin as we move in confession and repentance. As a result, we become much more eager to look within and deal with any issue that maybe taking away our inner peace, which is a promise of the New Covenant (see John 14:27). Like the heart of David, we willingly look into our own hearts so we can walk right with G-d; we want nothing to come between us, nothing to stand in the way of peace, faith, and most important of all the love of G-d that is operating deeply from within us. As Rabbi Paul put it, *"Everything that does not come from faith is sin"* (Romans 14:23), which can be any number of inner attitudes of our hearts that may take us out of faith and out of our peace that the New Covenant so masterfully provides, which is a great indicator as to whether our hearts are right with Him or not. Pride, anger, hatred, jealousy, unforgiveness, fear, doubt, control, being critical or judgmental are just a few of the conditions that can operate through our hearts that are sinful. Yet the wonder of the New Covenant is that because Yeshua paid the price for all of our sins, we can immediately be free of these through confession and repentance, which are actually incredible gifts from G-d—assuming we are not being hypocritical, of course, as G-d sees every attitude in our hearts.

Sin now no longer has any hold on us. When we operate with the New Covenant kingdom principles, which actually become incredibly empowering, He frees us from the emotional chains of our own hearts. As I moved more in these principles, as soon as something took me out of my peace and I felt it in my heart, I either asked G-d what happened, or I searched my own heart, recognizing it, and without any condemnation from G-d, I confessed it in prayer—and my peace returned to me. The total price for all of our sins has been paid, and there is absolutely no condemnation from G-d, as He has wiped us clean; and with confession, none of our sins are taken in to account. What counts in the New Covenant, is faith operating in love.

This brings me to my next point: G-d knew even beforehand that we Jews would fail Him in observing the Mosaic law, because He knew the condition of our hearts. In fact, I believe whoever He would have chosen would have made the same mistakes Israel did, because which human, or race, or nation of people are without the same sinful nature.

The Mosaic law had to be given to humankind, before He could send His Son to redeem us and He chose Israel for that purpose, as Rabbi Paul wrote that the law was put in charge to lead us to Messiah and it still operates today toward all mankind in order that we may know that our own sin separates us from a holy and righteous G-d (see Galatians 3:24; Matthew 5:17-18).

For what is the first thing that a new believer does when they accept Yeshua? They confess their sins; and without the law being in place, how would we know this? For when we accept Yeshua, we actually become free of the Old Covenant and immediately receive the new law into our hearts (the law of the Spirit of Life), the Holy Spirit who incorporates much of the truth of the Mosaic law into the New Covenant—except, now it is applied in a new way of the Spirit. For truth does not change, just as G-d does not change, except we are made new, being born from the Spirit of G-d. There is an incredible connection and transformation here between the Old and the New, for G-d has taken the truth and the Spirit from the Word of G-d and brought it into a New Covenant that is both living and active within us, as I have already stated, our hearts get circumcised with the very Spirit and law of G-d.

As Rabbi Paul says in Romans 8:4 that now, "the righteous requirement of the law might be fully met in us, who do not live according to the flesh [sinful nature], but according to the Spirit," for this is the new code. We have to become aware of the sinful state of our hearts first so that we can become free from the law and return to G-d (see Ephesians 2:14-18). However, as a result, the main purpose of the law did not actually bring life, as G-d used it to expose sin; as a result of officially bringing sin to life, it also brought its condemnation, as sin will ultimately be judged. As a result, we were all in need of a final redemption process, which was G-d's ultimate plan, to send His own Son (see Romans 7:4-8:4).

This is why G-d sent Yeshua at the end of the law, to take on its punishment and redeem us to bring us back to G-d. In so doing, He further established the Davidic Covenant upon the earth to prepare the seat of David upon His return to Jerusalem as King. His first coming was to be a suffering lamb; but when He returns, He will come like a roaring Lion to establish His kingdom on the earth! (See Revelation 19:11-18.)

For what the world has not fully realized is that Israel has not only suffered the consequences of the law for themselves, but also for all humankind. For the law was to be given solely to His first-born children with the task of facing the human heart against the Word of G-d. And because of our resistance and failure, it brought judgment, because despite our humanity, where there was law, there also had to be accountability.

Gentile believers were brought into the New Covenant afterward, as it was always G-d's plan to do so and Yeshua's sacrifice was a final payment for all humankind's sin; all can now be redeemed through His life, which was the Father's gift to humanity. Yet the law had to be given before Messiah could be sent, and Israel was called to face its consequences so that sin could be brought into account (see Romans 5:13), which has caused us immeasurable suffering. In addition, the Church has never really properly understood this, otherwise they would feel much more indebted toward the Jewish people for the price they have paid for all of us. However, just because He chose to work the law through our hearts, it did not excuse us from the consequences of not living in obedience to it. Just as Moses clearly pointed out, both the blessings and the curses of the covenant, we would still be responsible to uphold it and also suffer the consequences of our failure to keep it (see Deuteronomy 28–32).

It does not matter how much we really wanted to be like the other nations around us, G-d had already called us out, and as a result we had no choice in the matter, because He is G-d! The law was given to us, and we were therefore responsible to keep it. It brought about a standard that needed to be held. For we must understand that G-d is sovereign, in the words of Derek Prince, a British pastor who has truly loved the Jewish people and understood G-d's heart toward Israel, "G-d does what He wants, the way He wants, when He wants and He asks no one for permission."

Think for a moment of how authority actually works in our world today, as rules parents might lay down for their children. If the children do not obey, then the parents take action against them, to help them to get it right for the future. Think of the company you may work for, it establishes rules and regulations that you have to follow. What happens when you don't follow those rules? This is how authority works, laws get laid down and if they are not followed, action is naturally taken against those who break them.

G-d was incredibly patient with our people, both extremely long-suffering and forbearing. However, we only have to read the accounts in the Tenach (from Joshua to Malachi) to realize our own people's resistance to Him, even as He constantly held out His hand for us to turn back to Him, but we were not willing. In fact, right after Joshua dies and the Judges' reign is established over Israel, read what it says in Judges 2:10-11:

> *After that whole generation had been gathered to their ancestors, another generation grew up who knew neither the L-rd, nor what He had done for Israel. Then the Israelites did evil in the eyes of the L-rd and served the Baals.*

How quickly we departed from faith and obedience. We wanted to be like the other nations and follow their gods. We never really wanted the responsibility of the firstborn, and we looked to run from it instead.

In reading most of the Hebrew Scriptures, one can clearly see how the various books tell the story of Israel's struggles and disobedience to G-d. And while He always promised to restore us, we would ultimately face G-d's judgment as a result of our own sin and disobedience. This was certainly the case, by the time that G-d directs Isaiah to seal the veil over our people and here we finally see that G-d has lost patience with us. Everything is in our own Scriptures for us to read, if we would only take the time to look, it may be startling.

Read about Judah's dispersion to Babylon, where the great prophet Daniel lived, who has foretold us of the end times before the Messiah returns. Read about the prophet Hosea, whom G-d had marry a prostitute to show Israel how filthy she had become. Our right to live in the land is based upon righteousness that ultimately must reflect G-d's own character, which only the New Covenant can truly bring about.

One king after another did evil in the sight of G-d (see 1 and 2 Kings), which is why He then sent the prophets, so the authorities would be confronted—but they were also chased down and some of them were even killed. Only a handful of the kings of Judah and of Israel actually did right in G-d's eyes and by then much of the damage had been done. Both the people of Israel and Judah worshiped idols and other gods, and we compromised the law of G-d; the heart of our G-d was grieved by our actions against Him.

Yeshua told a story of a landowner.

"There was a landowner who planted a vineyard. He put a wall around it, dug a winepress in it and built a watchtower. Then he rented the vineyard to some farmers and moved to another place. When the harvest time approached, he sent his servants to the tenants to collect his fruit. The tenants seized his servants; they beat one, killed another, and stoned a third. Then he sent other servants to them, more than the first time, and the tenants treated them the same way. Last of all, he sent his son to them. 'They will

respect my son,' he said. But when the tenants saw the son, they said to each other, 'This is the heir. Come, let's kill him and take his inheritance.' So they took him and threw him out of the vineyard and killed him. Therefore, when the owner of the vineyard comes, what will he do to those tenants? 'He will bring those wretches to a wretched end,' they replied, 'and he will rent the vineyard to other tenants, who will give him his share of the crop at harvest time.'" Jesus said to them, "Have you never read in the Scriptures: 'The stone the builders rejected has become the cornerstone; the Lord has done this, and it is marvelous in our eyes'? Therefore I tell you that the kingdom of God will be taken away from you and given to a people who will produce its fruit. Anyone who falls on this stone will be broken to pieces; anyone on whom it falls will be crushed." When the chief priests and the Pharisees heard Jesus' parables, they knew he was talking about them. They looked for a way to arrest him, but they were afraid of the crowd because the people held that he was a prophet (Matthew 21:33-46).

In addition, we must be willing to look at the circumstances that have transpired with our own people, so we can properly address them. While a good number of us are currently enjoying prosperity and the fruits of our hard work, for the most part, our people have suffered greatly over the centuries finding rejection and great persecution almost wherever we went. In fact many of us, not knowing why all of this has actually transpired, have often spoken back to G-d and asked Him to choose somebody else. After all, if we are G-d's chosen people, why have we suffered so? And the question is fair without true and in-depth knowledge of G-d's Word, which many secular Jews don't know that much about.

In the movie *Fiddler on the Roof*, the main character, Tevye, asks this very same question and many of us relate to this, because of what our people have suffered. However, this Diaspora, which may have been the longest, was not the first one. We learn from reading the

Scriptures, as I have already briefly mentioned, that our people were dispersed twice before, the Israelites to Assyria and Judah to Babylon. In both cases, we learn that the people's right to remain in the land was based upon their holiness and obedience to G-d, and indeed we were cast out because of our own actions. Just look at what the prophet Jeremiah wrote about before Judah was exiled to Babylon (see Jeremiah chapters 16, 17).

However, with every warning and judgment about us written in His Word, there are also comforting words and future promises to us, despite our own resistance, that He will ultimately restore us—that we would still come into our priestly calling, which is to be a holy people and a light to the world, which I believe is still to take place, and much sooner than we may think (see Isaiah 61:6-8).

If all of the Scriptures concerning the reestablishment of Israel had already been fulfilled with Israel's restoration to the land in 1948 and now we had just witnessed the fulfillment in G-d's word concerning the Jewish people being re-gathered from the North, from the former Soviet Union (see Jeremiah 16:14,15), where then are the rest of G-d's first-born children in G-d's overall plan for humanity? Why did G-d choose Israel in the first place, and why have our people suffered so much in light of this call?

While I believe I have some answers to these questions, I am not G-d and as a human have only a limited understanding into the way He thinks and operates. However, as it says in Torah, *"The secret things belong to the L-rd our G-d, but the things revealed belong to us and to our children forever, that we may follow all the words of this law"* (Deuteronomy 29:29). In other words, we have His Holy Word to direct us and through it we can see much of what G-d wants us to understand. However, we must be willing to face some difficult issues in this process, if we truly want to be able to move forward with our

G-d who loves us with an everlasting love, but who will not compromise His holiness or character for our mistakes—and thank G-d that He will not. After all, if He is G-d, is He not sovereign to lay down His own plans for us; and if we choose not to accept them, are we then not responsible for the consequences? Is this not in fact what Moses warned us about in the blessings and the curses writings in the Torah? (See Deuteronomy 28-31.)

For if we are truly honest with ourselves, our people were cast out of our own land as a result of our disobedience to G-d and have we not paid a great price as a result? For while G-d's love is poured out for all those who obey Him, to a thousand generations of those who love Him (see Exodus 20:6), what happens to us when we fall outside of His grace and protection? Have we truly forgotten the power of G-d who not only took us out of Egypt with great signs and wonders, but also delivered the land of Canaan into our hands with an incredible anointing that was upon us?

Did not the nations shake in their shoes because of the fear of the L-rd that was upon us wherever we went? And who was it that gave our people all of the victories we experienced in moving into the Promised Land and establishing the nation of Israel, if not G-d Himself? Are we indeed not like the prophet Habakkuk who could not understand how G-d would allow the Babylonians, a heathen nation, to bring judgment on the people of Judah because of their disobedience? (See Habakkuk chapters 1–2.)

It is even more difficult for us to consider that if G-d does exist, why would He allow us to suffer and not intervene on our behalf? Indeed, the lack of G-d's intervention to protect our people through the Holocaust became the main reason why Jewish people began to move away from their religious base, because we could not understand or even grasp how this could have happened. When one operates from a humanistic point of view, this kind of thinking is understandable. But G-d has another plan and His ways are not like ours, nor is He a humanist, as humanism seeks to eliminate G-d's sovereignty over us.

We need to be very careful here how we actually think of ourselves in light of any comparison to the Creator of the universe. Yet, we must learn from our past, as well as our own actions as a people, because in reality, we actually came out from under G-d's protection of us; and as a result, the devil has been able to come against us in his many attempts to try to eliminate us from the earth.

The Holocaust was never G-d's desire for us, but rather a satanic plan that was able to both seduce and work its way through the wickedness of humankind's nature. Just the thought alone of one man treating another like we were treated in those camps was nothing short of diabolical. Yet, in it we can see how low man can actually go to keep his own power and control over the earth, heaven help us!

For what we have not really understood is that we are a covenant people, and G-d keeps His promises and His Word through us. In order for Messiah to return, we must be restored, both physically and spiritually as a people, just as His Word predicts, which is why the devil hates us so much and wants to destroy us. For while G-d knew we would be dispersed, He also knows that we will be ultimately redeemed just as He has promised. However, if the devil can stop this from happening, he can deny the power and truth of G-d and keep dominion over the earth, or so he thinks.

For what we don't really know as Jews, because it is revealed to us in the New Testament (Revelation 20–21), is that when Yeshua returns to establish His throne in Jerusalem, the devil will be finished, so his defeat is also based upon our spiritual restoration. As a result, there is a battle that goes on in the heavenly realm, and our people are right at the center of it, whether we like it or not.

Ultimately this is not really about us (even though it is), but about G-d keeping His covenants to us, which is why it is so important for us to be able to try to understand more of how G-d actually operates. This may sound crazy, especially when you look at the world from such a secular viewpoint, but we must awaken to the fact that we are more than dust and that our spirits will live forever—and indeed that the spiritual world has much more influence over us than we actually think or even know.

Like it says in Ezekiel:

"Therefore say to the Israelites, 'This is what the Sovereign L-rd says: It is not for your sake, people of Israel, that I am going to do these things, but for the sake of my holy name, which you have profaned among the nations where you have gone. I will show the holiness of my great name, which has been profaned among the nations, the name you have profaned among them. Then the nations will know that I am the L-rd,' declares the Sovereign L-rd, 'when I am proved holy through you before their eyes. 'For I will take you out of the nations; I will gather you from all the countries and bring you back into your own land.' "…I am not doing this for your sake," declares the sovereign L-rd. "Be ashamed and disgraced for your conduct, people of Israel" (Ezekiel 36:22-24,32).

In other words, G-d's plans will come to pass, despite ourselves, or even our own resistance to Him; like G-d said, we should be ashamed because of the way we have acted toward our own G-d and humiliated Him, because we are His firstborn, and therefore represented His presence and character on the earth—and look what we did with it.

However, out of all the horror and the destruction in those concentration camps, our own nation was reborn and out of our death and suffering came new life, just like Yeshua's death and resurrection. For G-d showed this very thing to Ezekiel twenty-five hundred years prior to its happening in chapter 37—for Israel was to come forth again from the dry bones of the Holocaust.

As I have already mentioned, while I cannot fully explain this or even put it into words, there is definitely some correlation between the sufferings of Messiah and the sufferings of His firstborn, a burden and a yoke that is not on any other group or type of people, that we His firstborn have borne for the world.

Yet out of all of this is coming the fulfillment of G-d's plan to both restore and redeem us, except He chose first to put us back in the land before He would cleanse us from our sins, which can only come through the New Covenant. It is only a question of G-d's timing to restore us spiritually to Himself, and this must happen before Messiah can return.

Just look at the second part of Ezekiel 36:

I will sprinkle clean water on you, and you will be clean; I will cleanse you from all of your impurities and from all of your idols. I will give you a new heart and put a new spirit in you; I will remove from you your heart of stone and give you a heart of flesh. And I will put my Spirit in you and move you to follow my decrees and be careful to keep my laws. Then you will live in the land I gave your ancestors; you will be my people and I will be your G-d (Ezekiel 36:24-28).

In the meantime however, most of us have moved into a secular direction concerning our faith. Still deeply holding to our roots, our heritage, and our traditions, but not really having any personal relationship and intimacy with our Creator, like Abraham had. At best, fewer of us are still religious, and most of us are agnostic, still acknowledging the existence of a higher power, but not really knowing Him, and a number of us don't even believe in G-d anymore.

Up until the retaking of Jerusalem by Israel in 1967, we Jews have not had much choice in our spiritual connection, ranging from ultra-Orthodox to conservative and liberal theology, which is mostly supported by secular Jews. However, this recapturing of Jerusalem definitely affected a change in the heavenly realm toward the Jewish people. At the very same time, the Messianic movement was born, and all of a sudden many younger modern Jews started once again to come to faith in Yeshua and found reconnection with their G-d, despite all of the barriers and opposition.

This was the beginning of the fulfillment of the second part of Ezekiel's prophecies in chapters 36 and 37, where the Spirit of G-d is breathed back into Israel. This immediately gave those first Messianic Jews both an intimate and personal relationship with their G-d, which they could not deny. Just like Jeremiah had said, that we would all know G-d for ourselves (see Jeremiah 31:34), which can only happen through Messiah. As I personally testified earlier in the book, when I came to faith and accepted Yeshua, it was as if a spiritual veil was lifted from my soul and all of a sudden my eyes were opened and now I could see and feel G-d for myself.

As a result, our options over the past two thousand years have actually been quite limited, and it is no great surprise that most modern Jews have moved away from the heavy religious burden, because its practices were not only archaic, but also brought us into legalistic bondage rather than spiritual freedom.

Orthodox Judaism, which still places a heavy religious burden upon us, reflects an old and legalistic approach to the law, which was changed by the rabbis because we could no longer sacrifice without the existence of the Temple. We also neglected to see this as a sign when it was destroyed. After all, if the G-d of heaven and earth had given us the Mosaic law and the sacrificial system, why would He take it away from us if we were supposed to continue with it? It was then replaced by a system of works in the study of G-d's word to the point now where the Talmud[3] is often esteemed over the prophetic writings of the scripture, bringing even greater legalism.

However, when we go back into biblical times, we can see that the heart of the law was justice, mercy, and faithfulness. And G-d had required mercy over sacrifice (see Hosea 6:6). Yet because of man's weakness to control, we became extremely legalistic in our approach, putting our own observances over the heart of the law, which allowed spiritual pride to enter into the hearts of our leaders and caused them to be deceived.

As modern Jews, we have never really had the opportunity to understand G-d's full picture and plan for humankind, as we got caught into the system of the law and then moved further into the world because of the Holocaust. And although G-d gave us His holy law, it was never meant to be the ending system, but rather a bridge to bring us to a final and complete redemption. As a result, Judaism continued to reflect the heavy legalistic burden of the law instead of bringing us into the New Covenant where Yeshua would place the law in our hearts.

Part 3: Our Future Destiny

Everything that has happened to us has also been foretold, including our suffering (see Deuteronomy 28). However, what most of the Church failed to see, that Rabbi Paul pointed out to Gentile believers in his letter to the Romans (9-11), was that G-d was not finished with us. The spiritual hardening that G-d placed upon us through Isaiah (6:8-10), was like a sealing off for another future time in humankind's history when G-d would once again use His firstborn, Israel, to show forth His glory to the nations (see Ezekiel 36). I do not even need to make mention of the prophecies in the Hebrew Scriptures that foretold the reestablishment of the land, because they have already miraculously taken place. In fact, almost every prophecy concerning us has already happened from Abraham up until this modern day, and only a few are actually left to be fulfilled; just read for yourselves.

What is it about this tiny bit of real estate, a little larger than the State of New Jersey, that makes the whole world want it? It really has to be a spiritual issue when you think about it, as nothing else really makes any sense! I cannot find a better teaching to point out the fact that what G-d has said and written concerning Israel and the Jewish people without any doubt will come to pass, than Derek Prince's teachings on Israel. Listen to what he said, "For Israel's entire history was foretold in prophecy, which is not true of any other nation." It is really important for us as Jews to both realize and understand this, as it may help us to see that there is actually great spiritual significance to the fact that we are born of Jewish decent. For we must come to learn that the G-d of Israel still wants to work out His will through us, so that He may show His glory to all of the nations on the earth in keeping His words and covenants to Israel.

One thing in my life that I knew now that I could count on is that the G-d of Israel is faithful. G-d has been so misunderstood because the world is blind to His ways as a result of sin. Also, the devil has been all over end-time theology, so there is much confusion about it, many different understandings about the end days before Messiah returns.

Derek Prince breaks down these prophecies into sixteen predictions.[4] It is very important for us to see how Scripture is really true when it comes to our people regarding what has already happened and what is still to take place. Take a good look at these prophecies, most of which have already been fulfilled:

The first three were given to Abraham:

1. The prediction of their enslavement in Egypt for 400 years (Genesis 15:12-14)

2. The deliverance with wealth from Egypt; this literally happened overnight as they plundered the Egyptians (Genesis 15:12-14)

3. The possession of the land of Canaan (Genesis 17:8)

4. That Israel would turn to idolatry in the Promise land (Deuteronomy 28)

5. G-d would establish a center of worship in Jerusalem (2 Samuel 7)

6. That the Northern Kingdom [Israel] would be carried into captivity in Assyria (Isaiah 8:4)

7. That the Southern Kingdom (Judah) would be carried into captivity into Babylon (Habakkuk)

8. The destruction of the first Temple, built by Solomon (Zephaniah)

9. The return of a small Remnant from Babylon (Jeremiah)

10. The destruction of the second Temple (Matthew 24:1,2)

11. Jewish people to be scattered because of disobedience (Leviticus 26)

12. That Israel would endure persecution and oppression among the Gentiles (Deuteronomy 28)

13. That Israel would be re-gathered by all nations; this is happening now (Ezekiel 36)

14. The gathering of all nations in war against Jerusalem (Zechariah)

15. The supernatural revelation of Messiah to His people; this has begun, but there will also be a national repentance (Zechariah 12:10-12)

16. The coming of Messiah to establish His kingdom in glory and power upon the earth (Isaiah, Revelation)

So far thirteen out of sixteen have been fulfilled that were all predicted before they happened. This is approximately 81%, so I don't think that we would have to be crazy fanatics to believe that the remaining three will actually come to pass and be fulfilled, do you? To me it's logical to think that if a book can predict thirteen events in advance with correctness and accuracy, any other predictions in that book should be taken pretty seriously and indeed Israel must fully come into its position in order for Messiah to return. This much I am certain of, it is only just a question of G-d's timing on the earth.[5]

Don't ask me why G-d chose to bring our people back to the land without cleansing us spiritually first, He obviously has His purposes, but as I mentioned when we took back Jerusalem in 1967, the spiritual awakening began, and many Jews started to believe in Yeshua for the first time since the first century—coincidence or design? Look what will happen to our people in *"that day"* as we draw closer to Messiah's return. See what the prophet Zechariah wrote?

...They will look on me, the one they have pierced and they will mourn for him as one mourns for an only child and grieve bitterly for him, as one grieves for a firstborn son. On that day the weeping in Jerusalem will be great, like the weeping of Hadad Rimmon in the plain of Megiddo. The land will mourn, each clan by itself with their wives by themselves... (Zechariah 12:10-12).

We will then realize the tragedy of our own error. Can you believe the clearness of this word back to our people, from our own prophet? One can hardly believe this Scripture, but as we come down to the end, it actually makes perfect sense, as we Jews need to realize that we have actually made a great mistake but still have an amazing destiny to fulfill—and Yeshua cannot wait for this day to happen. He longs for us to return to Him so that all can be fulfilled and Messiah can return to the earth and reign with us as our Divine King. He will supernaturally lift that veil from all of our people who are willing to open their hearts to Him before He returns and we all will finally call upon Him, just as we all listened to Him that night in Egypt when we were passed over. In reality, both Jews and Christians are waiting for the same Messiah to return—and His name is *Yeshua!* When Yeshua returns, He will take His seat on David's throne and establish a thousand-year reign upon the earth (see Revelation 20:1-4) where truth and justice will be both seen and experienced throughout the earth, and the world will be changed forever. This may be hard to even imagine, but it will happen, because G-d's word will always come to pass, as well as all of the circumstances in order for it to take place.

Israel will finally come into its priestly role (see Exodus 19:6) and will rule the nations with the rest of G-d's believing family (see Revelation 5:9-10)—and then there will truly be peace upon the earth. I believe that we have already entered this prophetic age, evident with the numerous shakings and goings on in our current world, which are only going to increase. As G-d will not be mocked and the world is becoming increasingly wicked and self-seeking, as sin continues to draw us away from His grace and protection over us, it will have its consequences.

And don't think that the United States is necessarily a safe haven. If history has taught us anything, just look at Germany and how our people had reached the top of that society. If this current world economy topples, and it definitely seems like we are heading in that direction, who do you think they will blame? It unfortunately does not require much of an imagination to answer that question.

Everything is coming into place at the right time and G-d's body is moving toward us and is also experiencing their own awakening to reconnect with the people of Israel and the family of G-d. They will ultimately stand with us; the rest, however, will not. The book of Revelation tells us of an antichrist who will come to the earth before Messiah returns who, much like Hitler, will deceive the world. One thing I can assure you, he will be no friend of the Jews—and may deceive us at first.

The spiritual awakening of the Jews is additional testament to the current times we are living in; and while it may be in its infancy, it will eventually spread to all of those in Israel who will call upon His name, for His words and promises shall be fulfilled. Just as Rabbi Gamaliel said to the Sanhedrin in Jerusalem when the apostles first started moving in His power shortly after His resurrection, *"…But if it is from G-d, you will not be able to stop these men; you will only find yourselves fighting against G-d"* (Acts 5:33-39).

We received a hardening, and through it many in the Gentile world have come to faith. Now, before He returns, this veil will be lifted and finally our people will be cleansed from their sins and from within their hearts through the New Covenant in Yeshua. There are so many Scriptures that foretell this, and if G-d has already fulfilled much of His promises to us, why should we ever believe that this will not happen? Please read them for yourself: Deuteronomy 30:1-6; Isaiah 6:9-10, 29:9-14; Ezekiel 34:11-13, 36:24-38; Isaiah 43:5-9; Jeremiah 31:31-37; Zechariah 8; Micah 7:18-20.

As one who has now crossed over to the New Covenant and returned to the G-d of Israel, I wish you could understand how much

He really loves you, how intimately He wants to be with you in His own masterful, unique ways. How beautiful His peace feels as it sweeps through your soul; or how His love melts your heart with His goodness and His kindness even when He is gently correcting you; or His healing touch, as He promises to restore what the locusts have stolen and brings emotional and sometimes physical healing to your life. You just don't know what you are really missing until you get in touch with Him!

The New Covenant helps to reconnect us to G-d in a way that was similar to Abraham's call. He knew G-d intimately through faith, which we also need to have to believe, as indeed, this is the way that G-d has designed it. So much so that Abraham just picked up and left his home country owing to the voice and call of G-d, as well as his own faith in his heart. This is how it should be with us in our lives, being guided and directed personally by G-d.

Similarly, when you accept G-d's plan by accepting Yeshua, who is One with the Father (see John 14), G-d's Spirit will flood your heart and your soul, and for the first time in your life you will honestly know G-d for yourself.

Yeshua is not just an intermediary, He brings us straight into the throne room of G-d through the veil and directly into the Holy of Holies where the Father presides. It is evidenced by the reconnection that we can all feel in our own hearts, which He also confirms in the His Word, where Jeremiah said that we would all know G-d for ourselves (see Jeremiah 31:34).

What are you waiting for? We still have a destiny to fulfill to bring glory to the holy G-d of Israel and despite ourselves, He will do it and bring it to pass; it is only a question of time and history in order for these things to take place. For Yeshua will not return until we (Jews) have said, *"Blessed is He who comes in the name of the L-rd!"* (Matthew 23:39).

Don't wait until it is too late, when circumstances may not be as easy or as comfortable as they may be right now. Decide today so that you have time to reconnect and get to know G-d for yourself, to be built up in His holy Word and allow His Spirit to cleanse you and make you ready for the most exciting days that are ahead of us. Decide today so that we may all come into the ultimate destiny that was planned for us before the beginning of creation. Wow, how exciting is that?

Part 4: What Do You Have to Lose?

At the end of my search, Maria ultimately confronted me, "What do you have to lose? You are praying, you are talking to G-d. If Yeshua is the Messiah and G-d's Son, why don't you just ask Him?" When you think about this, really, it seems so simple; but look what we have been through as a people and it will help you understand why it is such a difficult prayer for any Jew to pray.

Nevertheless, if you have come this far in this book as a Jewish person, or as a Gentile, this is exactly what I am going to ask you to do. *What do you have to lose by asking your own G-d, the G-d of Abraham, if Yeshua is really the Messiah?* He could always say, *"No,"* if it is not so! However, if He is who He says He is, shouldn't we respond to Him? Is it possible that our leaders have made a tragic error, which could be one of the main reasons that the most religious among us are steeped in such legalism? Was this really G-d's intention? Yeshua has told us that His burden is light and His yoke is easy (see Matthew 11:30).

The heart of G-d is about love and mercy, not just sacrifice. One thing I can both promise and assure you of: when you step into the New Covenant, you will actually know G-d for yourself and He will never disappoint you. As strange as it may seem because of all of the deception, the division, and the persecution and suffering, the New

Covenant is the only true extension of Judaism. This is where G-d has led us, and if we truly want Him in our lives, we must be willing to yield to His plan and direction for us. Salvation for all peoples' souls comes from no other place than through Yeshua who greatly desires all to come to the knowledge of the truth.

If you are truly seeking, pray this prayer to G-d: *"L-rd G-d of Israel, please show me the truth about You. And if Yeshua is really your loving Son, please show me about Him, because I really want to know You personally in a way that You can come into my life and my heart and touch me with Your love and peace. Amen, in G-d's precious name I pray."*

If you are ready to accept Yeshua into your life, ask Him to come into your heart and confess your sins to Him. Ask Him for forgiveness and that He would make Himself known to you.

Please read the Bible. Start with Moses and the prophets, and if you can open your heart to the New Testament, Yeshua's teachings will blow you away. You will be extremely surprised by all that He said and taught. It will be like water for your soul, as it was and is for me every time I read His holy Word.

ENDNOTES

1. Dispensation: A certain order, system, or arrangement; administration or management. See Dictionary.com.

2. Sanhedrin: ancient Jewish council: the supreme Jewish judicial, ecclesiastical, and administrative council in ancient Jerusalem before AD 70, having 71 members from the nobility and presided over by the high priest; http://www.bing.com/Dictionary/search?q=define+Sanhedrin&qpvt=sanhedrin+definition&FORM=DTPDIA; accessed April 24, 2012.

3. Talmud: Has two main components; the Mishna and the Gemarah and is the summary of the oral law in thought and discussion that evolved after centuries of scholarly effort by Jewish sages who lived in Palestine and Babylonia. These works have been written and compiled over several centuries beginning in the sixth century BC up through the middle ages. www.lgrossman.com/mjnk/talmudsources.htm.

4. Derek Prince, *Why Israel,* Study notes CD4414. www.Derekprince.org.

5. Ibid.

Chapter 20

TO BE CONTINUED...

I was to come home that year from the Russian ministry to some incredible surprises and a whole new direction in my life. As I continued to mature in my relationship with G-d, the Holy Spirit started to lead me into deeper places in my personal walk with Him. These additional experiences brought on greater faith and dependency in my life, both in blessings as well as additional trials. All of which were to begin to prepare me for the next spiritual phase and plan of G-d for my life to help awaken my people.

I was to receive a fantastic offer for my business, our third child, Madison, was to be born, and the most exciting Spirit-led stories continued to open new doors to my life that I could not imagine and that only my adventures in the kingdom of G-d could reveal.

To be continued…

ABOUT THE AUTHOR

Grant Berry has been a Jewish believer in Yeshua, Jesus the Messiah since 1985. He is married to Donna Berry and has three children, Joshua, Jonathan, and Madison. For most of his spiritual life, he has been both an entrepreneur and a minister of the gospel. He has founded and built three cosmetic companies, as well as a number of ministries focused on reaching Jewish people, both in the U.S. under the Wilkerson brothers at Times Square Church, and in the former Soviet Union with Abraham's Promise, leading thousands of Jews and Gentiles to faith. *The New Covenant Prophecy* tells his spiritual journey.

Grant now leads a ministry in the New York area called Messiah's House, which is focused on uniting Jews and Gentiles into the New Covenant. He also leads Reconnecting Ministries and Products with a vision to awaken the Church into its end time destiny to help rebirth Israel in the Spirit of G-d.

Grant is available to teach on Reconnecting Israel and the Church and can be contacted through him Website at:

www.reconnectingministries.org.

IN THE RIGHT HANDS, THIS BOOK WILL CHANGE LIVES!

Most of the people who need this message will not be looking for this book. To change their lives, you need to put a copy of this book in their hands.

> *But others (seeds) fell into good ground, and brought forth fruit, some a hundred-fold, some sixty-fold, some thirty-fold* (Matthew 13:8).

Our ministry is constantly seeking methods to find the good ground, the people who need this anointed message to change their lives. Will you help us reach these people?

> *Remember this—a farmer who plants only a few seeds will get a small crop. But the one who plants generously will get a generous crop* (2 Corinthians 9:6).

EXTEND THIS MINISTRY BY SOWING
3 BOOKS, 5 BOOKS, 10 BOOKS, **OR MORE TODAY,** AND BECOME A LIFE CHANGER!

Thank you,

Don Nori Sr., Founder
Destiny Image
Since 1982

DESTINY IMAGE PUBLISHERS, INC.

"Promoting Inspired Lives."

VISIT OUR NEW SITE HOME AT
WWW.DESTINYIMAGE.COM

FREE SUBSCRIPTION TO DI NEWSLETTER

Receive free unpublished articles by top DI authors, exclusive
discounts, and free downloads from our best and newest books.

Visit www.destinyimage.com to subscribe.

Write to: Destiny Image
              P.O. Box 310
              Shippensburg, PA 17257-0310

Call: 1-800-722-6774

Email: orders@destinyimage.com

For a complete list of our titles or to place an order
online, visit www.destinyimage.com.

FIND US ON FACEBOOK OR FOLLOW US ON TWITTER.

www.facebook.com/destinyimage   facebook
www.twitter.com/destinyimage   twitter